The Golf Rules
Problem Solver

The Golf Rules Problem Solver

Steve Newell

COLLINS & BROWN

First published in 2005 by Chrysalis Books Group
The Chrysalis Building
Bramley Road
London W10 6SP

An imprint of **Chrysalis** Books Group plc

Copyright © 2005 Chrysalis Books Group
Text copyright © 2005 Steve Newell
Front cover image © Phil Sheldon Golf Picture Library
All commissioned photography by Angus Murray
Photographed on location at Brocket Hall Golf Club, Herfordshire

1 3 5 7 9 8 6 4 2

ISBN: 1 84340 194 0

Commissioning editor: Chris Stone
Designer: Phil Clucas
Reproduction by Classic Scan Pte Ltd
Printed and bound by SNP Leefung Printers Limited in China

Contents

Introduction

Golf, more than any other game, is a truly self-governing pastime and thus in no other sport is there a greater onus on participants to know, understand and abide by the rules. The game is infinitely more enjoyable, not to mention fairer, if everyone plays by the same rules. It is these rules which unite golfers of all standards. The weekend player, the red-hot amateur, the struggling tour pro and the world No. 1 – each and every one of them must play the same game, give or take a few special considerations regarding grandstands and the like in pro tournaments, even if the numbers at the bottom of the score card bear little resemblance.

The trouble is, at golf courses around the world there are occasionally signs of a worrying lack of rule-awareness – not through deliberate dishonesty but rather through ignorance. Regrettably few golfers are introduced to the rules of golf when they take up the game, while more experienced golfers get by on a handful of rudimentary rules, but unconsciously come to grief simply by following procedures that might seem logical, convenient and correct, but sadly are not.

Whatever the reasons, the heart of the matter is that golf is self-governing and it is therefore the golfer's duty to know the rules. While there are a good many to understand these days, a sound knowledge of the rules of golf does not require protracted study or prodigious memory.

There is an enormous degree of overlap within the rules, with certain relief procedures applying to many different sets of circumstances. Providing key elements are mastered, 99 percent of every round of golf played will present very few dilemmas. Even on the rare occasion when a problem is encountered, a little lateral thinking on the part of the rule-aware golfer is usually enough to overcome the difficulty and provide an equitable solution.

Like so much in life, it used to be simpler. In 1744, when the Honourable Company of Edinburgh Golfers, officially recognised as the oldest golf club in the world, penned on one side of paper the first Rules of Golf, there were only 13 of them – and rather odd some of the rules were, too. There was no such thing as marking the ball – if an opponent's ball was in your way, you had to putt around it or find a way over it. The 'stymie' was one of the many bizarre rules that was doomed to be ditched when the Royal & Ancient took over the running of the game in the mid-19th century. Since then the rule book has grown considerably, jointly presided over by the Royal & Ancient, based at St Andrews, in Scotland, the home of golf, and the United States Golf Assocation (USGA), based in New Jersey. Together, these two organisations efficiently govern a game that is continually changing, growing and evolving in subtle, but meaningful, ways.

The aim of *The Golf Rules Problem Solver* is not to usurp the R&A and USGA's authority and establish a new code of conduct, but rather to support the rules while making them more understandable. The intimidating, rather dry and lifeless text so often associated with rule books is largely gone and in its place comes a more user-friendly approach – a plain-language guide to all the key rules that every golfer should know. Not only does this book bring the rules to life, it should also bring them into clearer focus. Designed to accompany the golfer on the course, it highlights key points in the clearest possible way, serving as companion and arbiter.

The book also features a series of Pro Tips designed to help golfers gain a strategic edge...all within the rules, of course. Also scattered liberally throughout the book are Problem Solver tips, designed to clarify tricky and possibly ambiguous on-course scenarios, which might cause unwary golfers to...well, perhaps come a cropper!

Tucked away in the pocket of the golf bag, this book can be called upon whenever required to settle contentious, possibly score-wrecking, predicaments. Unlike the professional, the amateur golfer will not have a referee on hand to provide guidance whenever a query occurs. Being a self-governing game, the onus is on golfers to be aware of the rules to ensure that all play on the same terms.

It's been that way for 250 years and it's the way ahead.

Steve Newell

Important definitions

The whole concept of this section may seem basic, but it's a big mistake to think you can skip by it – even if you're well beyond the novice phase. The thing is, much of the essential golfing terminology relating to the rules can be a little unusual, so a familiarity with these definitions will make it a lot easier to understand the rules themselves.

Addressing the ball You've officially addressed the ball when you have taken your stance and also grounded the club. So if your ball is perched precariously on tall grass, loose chippings or pine needles, it's wise to hover the clubhead at address *(right)* because the ball could easily move and, if you ground the club, you will be penalised. Remember, though, you can't ground your club in a hazard, such as a bunker, so in those situations you are deemed to have addressed the ball the moment you take your stance.

Advice There are strict rules applying to this, so it is worth knowing what it constitutes. Advice is any counsel or suggestion which could influence a player in the choice of club or the way a certain shot is played. Crucially, however, any information relating to the rules of golf or on matters such as the position of a hazard or, say, where the flag is on the green, does not count as advice.

Ball in play A golf ball is in play as soon as you've made a stroke on the teeing ground. It remains in play until you have holed out, except when it is lost, out of bounds or lifted, or another ball has been substituted under an applicable rule. You can have only one ball in play at a time. So, if your ball heads off towards a water hazard and you then drop another ball and play it, the second ball is then officially in play. Should you find your original ball and play it, whether it was in a water hazard or not, you will have played the wrong ball.

Bunker This is described as a hazard consisting of a prepared area of ground, often a hollow, from which turf or soil has been removed and replaced with sand or the like. Grass-covered ground bordering or within the bunker is not part of the bunker, so you can ground your club in those areas. The margin of a bunker extends vertically downward, but not upward.

Caddie Nice if you can get one, but here's the official line. A caddie is one who carries or handles your clubs during play and otherwise assists you in accordance with the rules.

Casual water This is defined as any temporary accumulation of water on the course which is visible before, or after, you take your stance. Obviously it doesn't count if you're up to your waist in a water hazard! Snow and ice are either casual water or a loose impediment, the choice is yours. Frost, however, is neither and does not entitle you to relief.

Committee The committee in charge of competitions is, in everyday golf clubs, unlikely to be on site at weekends. In these instances the club professional is usually authorised to act on behalf of the tournament committee.

Competitor A simple word with subtle, but crucial, variations in meaning. A competitor is a player in a strokeplay competition – so, that's you in the monthly medal. A fellow competitor is the person you play with in the monthly medal or indeed any other strokeplay event. Neither of you are partners and you certainly aren't playing partners. It may sound pedantic, but confusion as to the exact definition of the people in a group of golfers can cause problems with the rules.

Equipment This term applies to anything you use, wear or carry. Equipment also applies to your golf cart, motorised or not. The word 'equipment' does not apply to the ball being played, nor to any small objects such as ball-markers, coins or tees used, say, to indicate an area in which you are about to drop a ball.

Flagstick It's what you aim for and, sadly, seldom find. Its exact description is a 'movable straight indicator, with or without bunting or other material attached,' which explains why it isn't a problem that some golf clubs in the US have baskets instead of flags atop the flagsticks. It must be centred in the hole, though, and it has to be circular in cross-section.

Ground under repair This is defined as any part of the course so marked by the committee. It includes material piled for collection. It also includes any hole made by the greenskeeper, even if not so marked. The lines indicating ground under repair count as such, so if your ball is only just touching the line it counts as lying in ground under repair and you are entitled to free relief. Likewise, if you have to stand within ground under repair you are entitled to relief. It's important to note, however, that loose grass cuttings which are not obviously to be removed do not count as ground under repair.

Hazard Simple. Any bunker or water hazard. Avoid them at all costs!

Hole The rules are very specific concerning hole size. It must be 4.25in (10.8cm) in diameter and at least 4in (10cm) deep. If a lining is used, it must be sunk at least 1in (2.5cm) below the surface of the green.

Holed Your ball is only considered holed when it is at rest within the circumference of the hole and the whole ball is below the level of the lip.

Left: Bunkers strike fear into the hearts of many club golfers, but in actual fact they offer easier shots than they appear. A bunker shot is the only shot in golf where one deliberately attempts to not hit the ball, instead contacting the sand first.

Honour A very noble term, but it simply refers to the golfer entitled to play first from the teeing ground. This can be decided on the toss of a coin on the first tee, or the order of the draw sheet, and from thereon is determined by the player with the lowest score on the preceding hole.

Lateral water hazard This is one definition that becomes far clearer when you get to the rule itself. A lateral water hazard is one that is situated in such a way that it is not practical to drop a ball behind the hazard. You'll know when you're in one because it will be marked by red lines or stakes.

Line of play This is the direction you wish the ball to take after you've played the stroke, plus a reasonable distance on either side of the intended direction. The line of play extends vertically upward from the ground but, importantly, it does not extend beyond the hole.

Line of putt Much the same as the previous definition, only this time it applies specifically to the actual putting green. The line of a putt includes a reasonable distance either side of the intended line, but again it does not extend beyond the hole.

Loose impediments This term applies to natural objects such as stones, leaves, twigs, branches or insects and worms. They must not be growing objects, though, and they must not be fixed or solidly embedded. If it is stuck to your ball it cannot be described as a loose impediment. One tricky issue worth bearing in mind is that sand and loose soil are loose impediments on the green, but not elsewhere.

Lost ball This is one definition that may sound blindingly obvious, but there's more to it than meets the eye. A ball is lost if it is not found or identified by you within five minutes of beginning your search. A ball is also lost if you put another ball into play under the rules, even though you might not have searched for it. Likewise if you play a provisional ball from a point where the original ball is likely to be, or from a position beyond that point, then the provisional ball is the ball in play. Your original ball is, therefore, officially lost.

Move or moved This definition is measured in fractions. If your ball leaves its position and comes to rest in any other place, it is considered to have moved. If, however, you are playing golf on an exceptionally windy day and the ball merely oscillates, that does not count as moved. Neither does it count as having moved if the face of your putter just touches the ball as you address it, provided of course it doesn't actually shift position.

Obstruction This term applies to anything artificial that could get in the way of play. It includes tee markers, artificial surfaces and the sides of roads and paths. There are exceptions to this rule, though. The word obstruction does not apply to objects defining out of bounds, such as stakes, railings or a wall. So although they are definitely artificial, if your ball comes to rest against an out-of-bounds post, it's tough – you can't move the post and neither can you take a free drop. Also, some artificial objects can be declared an integral part of the course if the committee of the club so decides.

Above: Pop-up sprinkler heads are an immovable obstruction and, in this situation, the golfer would be entitled to relief without penalty.

Out of bounds The rules describe this as ground on which play is prohibited. When it is defined by stakes or a fence, the out of bounds line is determined by the nearest inside points of the stakes, fence or posts at ground level. But that doesn't include any angular supports.

Left: A ball cannot be played if it comes to rest beyond the margins of the white stakes indicating out of bounds.

When out of bounds is determined by a white line, the line itself is out of bounds. So if your ball is on that line, you're out of bounds. You can, however, stand out of bounds to play a ball resting within bounds.

Outside agency This applies to any agency that is not part of the match or, in stroke play, not part of the competitor's side. It includes a referee, a marker, an observer or a forecaddie (someone who is enlisted by the committee to spot balls during play). You can't claim wind or water as an outside agency.

Partner This is a player on the same side as you in, say, a foursome, a fourball or a betterball match. Remember the difference – even if you are playing with your best friend in a medal, he or she is not your partner.

Penalty stroke Not something that any golfer appreciates, but it's a fact of life on the course even for the greatest players in the world. There will be plenty of situations in this book describing the instances when penalty strokes are added to your score, or your side's score. If you play this game long enough, you are bound to become quite familiar with them.

Provisional ball This is an option you take when you suspect a ball may be lost outside a water hazard, or may be out of bounds. The key things to remember are that you can play a provisional ball in either strokeplay or matchplay, but you cannot play a provisional ball when you merely *suspect* your ball has finished in a water hazard. Make sure you state clearly your intentions, declaring out loud that you are about to hit a provisional ball before actually doing so.

Putting green Your ball is considered to be on the putting green when any part of it actually touches the green.

Rub of the green An unusual term that refers to a situation when a ball's motion is accidentally deflected or stopped by an outside agency. It can work both for and against you. Sometimes a rub of the green will deflect a poorly struck shot on to a green it otherwise wouldn't have hit. On other occasions a decent shot can be deflected out of bounds and you will have to accept that with equal grace.

Stance Taking your stance consists of you placing your feet in position for, and preparatory to, making a stroke.

Stipulated round This consists of playing the holes of the course in their correct sequence, unless otherwise authorised by the committee.

Right: A golf stroke must involve the actual intention of striking at, and thus physically moving, the ball.

Stroke The fewer you make, the better. The term 'stroke' describes the forward momentum of the club and must involve the intention of fairly striking at, and thus moving, the ball. This is why air shots count as strokes: you had every intention of moving the ball, but didn't. Don't forget, though, that if you manage to stop your swing halfway to the ball and before the clubhead actually reaches the ball, that doesn't count as a stroke.

Teeing ground This is where it all starts. Sometimes called a tee-box, it is a rectangular area two club-lengths in depth (it's up to you to measure that part if you want to utilise that space), the outside limits of which are defined by two tee-markers. Remember that you can stand outside the teeing ground as long as your ball is within it. You should always feel free to make use of those two club-lengths back from the

Right: The teeing ground is a closely mown area; and the ball must be teed between the margins of the two tee-markers.

markers – it has certain benefits, as we'll learn later in this book.

Through the green This is probably the single most misunderstood definition in the book. It does not apply to through the green, as in too long, but rather to the entire area of the golf course, except the tee and green of the hole being played and any hazard anywhere on the course. Don't let this one catch you out when looking up a ruling in the heat of battle.

Water hazard Different from the Lateral Water Hazard, it refers to any sea, lake, pond, river, ditch, surface drainage ditch or other open water course (whether or not it contains water), and anything of a similar nature. All ground or water within the margins of the water hazard is included as part of the water hazard. Even if you are on dry land within that hazard, don't take a practice swing which makes contact with the ground – that's a penalty. In case you are in any doubt about what type of hazard it is, water hazards are defined by yellow stakes or lines, as opposed to the red stakes or lines of a lateral water hazard. The relief procedures for the two types of water hazard do differ, and that will be dealt with later.

Wrong ball It's easy to play someone else's ball if you're careless when in deep rough. But believe it or not you can also play a wrong ball, owned by you, if you happen to transgress a few rules. Basically, a wrong ball is any ball other than the ball in play or a provisional ball. There is another instance in strokeplay whereby if you are unsure of a certain ruling you can play two balls on the affected hole, before then clarifying the ruling after your round. Under such circumstances you are in effect playing two balls, but you are not in theory playing a 'wrong' one.

Etiquette

One of the most famous sporting quotes includes the memorable passage that it matters not whether you win or lose, but how you play the game. This captures the essence of etiquette and it could hardly be more accurately applied than to the game of golf.

Etiquette encapsulates a variety of elements – good behaviour on the golf course, care for the golf course, personal integrity and, perhaps above all, consideration for one's playing partners and fellow competitors. The whole nature of the game as we know it depends on these codes of conduct being upheld.

Strangely, there is very little written on the subject in the official Rules of Golf; barely more than a paragraph, in fact. Etiquette comprises the largely unspoken, unwritten rules of behaviour, a fact that can cause concern as there is always a real danger that new generations of golfers joining the game will be unaware of the principles. Furthermore, experienced golfers basically have no real point of reference to etiquette other than word of mouth. If they happen to be in a group that is unfamiliar with these principles, then etiquette will possibly be lost on them, with significant repercussions.

If standards of etiquette are allowed to slide, then so gradually will the player's level of enjoyment. The experience of playing on even the most picturesque course can be almost completely ruined through the thoughtlessness and inconsiderate behaviour of others. Having the required equipment does not in itself make a golfer, and neither does having an elegant swing or shooting a low score. Good etiquette on the golf course is the mark of the true golfer – and of a popular one, too.

This section of the book is dedicated to outlining the key principles of etiquette and the reasons why it is so important to the whole fabric of the game of golf. It covers all the key elements a golfer should be aware of and is as important as are the Rules of Golf themselves.

Looking after the golf course

The benefits of looking after the golf course and ensuring that it is left in at least the condition in which you found it are not difficult to grasp. Regrettably, far too many golfers are either too lazy to do this, or are simply ignorant of the required 'courtesies.' It's important to look after the course, not just to ensure that it doesn't suffer from more wear and tear than is necessary, but also out of respect for those players who will be following you. The pitch mark you leave in the green, or the divot you leave unattended in the fairway, could spell the downfall of another player, or indeed your own on a future occasion.

Bunkers Most of us have enough trouble getting out of bunkers from a perfect lie in the sand, but when you step into a bunker and find your ball nestling in the size-10 FootJoy print of a player from an earlier group, it makes your task that much more difficult. What better motivation for not subjecting someone else to that depressing discovery. When you've finished in a bunker, use the rake provided *(left)* to smooth over the footprints and the divot-mark that you leave in the sand.

Pitch marks Putting surfaces are a greenskeeper's pride and joy; arguably no other part of the course receives such loving care and attention. Make sure you do your bit to maintain it at its best and that you don't subject the surface to the one thing that causes guaranteed long term damage, unrepaired pitch marks. Created when your ball lands on the green, these marks are completely harmless if they are repaired immediately. Left untended, though, that particular spot of the green can take weeks to recover. And,

Right: Pitch marks occur on all but the firmest of greens and cause no long-term damage, providing they are quickly repaired.

of course, they can impede the smooth run of the ball if some poor unfortunate happens to follow in your footsteps. Pitch marks are easy to repair, either with a tee-peg or a tool designed specifically for the job and which is available in any pro shop.

Other indentations We all want perfect putting surfaces to play on, but one of the things that can destroy them is golfers leaning heavily on their putters as they wait their turn. It's not such a serious issue on hard, links-style greens. But when the putting surfaces are soft and spongy, perhaps during the winter months or as a result of recent heavy rainfall, this careless practice can cause damage. So be mindful of this and try to avoid leaning heavily on your putter. You certainly wouldn't want your birdie putt veering off line at the last minute due to someone else's carelessness, so don't risk doing it to others.

Flagstick Even if you are feeling a little unhappy with your play, don't take it out on the flagstick or the green. When you remove the flagstick, place it gently on the ground, don't launch it javelin-style across the green.

Divots Good and bad shots alike can shift huge divots (*right*). Whether you're happy or ashamed of the shot that left its mark on the fairway, make sure you cover it up by replacing the divot. Just as unattended pitch marks cause long-term damage to the greens, so unreplaced divots can ruin a fairway, not to mention make it look very unattractive. Give it a good stamp into the ground to make sure it's securely in place before you set off towards the green.

Fill in divots on par-3s Soil-and-seed mixtures are often placed by the tee-markers on par-3s and this is considered the desired repair material, rather than replacing the actual divot you've just taken. This is not simply because the teeing ground will benefit in the long run, but because lots of loose divots in the same area (which is obviously bound to be the case on a teeing ground) can offer a pretty insecure footing for following golfers.

Mark your ball Before you putt out take a moment to assess whether in doing so you will have to tread on your playing partner's or fellow competitor's line to the hole. Footprints in themselves create no long-term damage, but they can leave indentations that last long enough to knock another ball off its natural line. If you are in any doubt, mark your ball with a small coin or a ball-marker and wait to putt out.

Above: Best to mark the ball with a small coin, or similar shaped object, as it is discreet enough to not become a distraction to other golfers as they putt.

Pro Tip

How to cope with those nasty footprints

We all know what a nightmare it is having to play a bunker shot from the footprints of a careless golfer who failed to rake the bunker. The circumstances will always vary, but as a general rule, aim to take a little more sand at impact and be extra-positive in your swing. If you try to play it like a normal bunker shot the ball often comes out too low and long, so try to remember that.

PROBLEM SOLVER

I was playing in a matchplay game last week when my opponent appeared to deliberately step on the line of my putt, damaging the green. Understandably I was annoyed, but since I didn't know the rules I didn't say anything. What could, or should, I have done?

You were right to be annoyed. This appears to be a case of poor etiquette of the highest order. Also, your opponent was in breach of the Rules of Golf. He should have immediately forfeited that hole, at the very least. The committee even has the right to disqualify him in such circumstances. Incidentally, if this happened in a strokeplay competition, the laws of equity would allow you to restore the green to its original condition – in other words, repair any damage made by your heavy-footed fellow competitor. The point is that any golfer is entitled to both the lie, and the line of putt, which he had when the ball first came to rest.

Respect for fellow competitors

The pleasure to be had from playing a round of golf can so easily turn sour through the rude or inconsiderate behaviour of others. Here is the indispensable guide to becoming a considerate and, ergo, a popular golfer.

Dress code If you're visiting a golf course for the first time, it's always wise to check the dress codes both inside the clubhouse and out. Jeans and T-shirts are not permitted at the majority of golf clubs. Training shoes are frequently frowned upon too, as are short socks worn with shorts. Some clubs will insist on a jacket and tie for lunch in the dining room, even on a very hot day, which can get visiting golfers literally hot under the collar. Whether you agree with it or not, try to be respectful.

Timekeeper Try to arrive on time for the games you've arranged. It may sound trivial, but some people find it quite stressful and certainly very off-putting if the last few minutes prior to teeing off in a competition are spent fretting about whether the final member, or indeed any other member, of the group is actually going to turn up.

You may not mind being a last-minute arrival, but try to make it to the tee in good time and remember that others could be unsettled by an anxious wait. Of course, should that be insufficient incentive, you may also want to keep in mind that you can be penalised if you turn up late and even disqualified.

Waiting your turn Stand in the correct position when you are waiting to tee off so as not to provide a distraction to the others playing in your group. It is generally felt that the best place to stand is to the right of the player teeing off, basically at an angle of 45 degrees to the target line. Stand still, too, because it's amazing how even the slightest movement can catch the corner of the eye and put players off their stroke.

Watch out Don't make practice swings in view of your fellow competitors or playing partners as they play or prepare to hit a shot; it's bound to distract them. Also, be careful of your practice swing – the clubhead can travel at speeds in excess of 100mph (160km/h) and golfers have been injured, even killed, through careless practice swings.

Above: Stand behind and slightly to the right while another golfer tees off.

Look out Keep an eye on the shots played by the golfers in your group, especially off the tee. If it looks as though it might hit someone, shout 'Fore!' ... loudly. And if you hit a shot into deep rough, even trees, try to mark the 'point of entry' with a distinguishing feature, something that will help you walk straight to the ball. Show some enthusiasm when helping your fellow competitors look for their ball; it's inconsiderate not to do so and also helps avoid slow play.

Pace of play A game of golf isn't supposed to be a race, but it isn't meant to be played at a crawl, either. Just as a slow driver can cause traffic jams, so it only takes one slow group of golfers to cause a backlog on the entire course. Make no mistake, slow play can be just as infuriating as any traffic jams. So it's important you make sure you know how to keep the pace of play moving along smoothly. It's very straightforward if you just remember a few guidelines.

Do call through the group behind if you can't find your ball immediately. Although the Rules of Golf allow you to look for a ball for five minutes, if you can't find your original ball immediately, the correct procedure is to wave the group behind to come through, provided of course they are ready to play. Ideally, you should also have played a provisional off the tee if you suspected your ball might be tough to find. That then saves you the additional delay of having to walk back to play another ball from the tee. It's amazing how these little delays add up.

Above: If a ball isn't immediately found, call through the group behind to avoid unduly delaying play, assuming of course they themselves are ready to play.

Don't hit unless you are sure the group ahead is out of range. You may be in a hurry, you may think the group in front is playing slowly, you may even be feeling impatient, but hitting a potentially lethal object

250 yards (228m) through the air into the vicinity of the players in front is best avoided. What may be your idea of a subtle reminder to the group in front to get a move on could easily have nasty consequences.

Do leave your golf bag on the correct side of the green, so that you can pick it up on the way past to the next tee. It doesn't take a lot of thought, and again it's amazing how those few saved seconds can add up over 18 holes.

Don't mark your card on the green of the hole you've just played – this is particularly annoying for those waiting to hit their approach shots. It must have happened to you, so don't put others through the same agony. Mark your card on the way to the next tee, or on the next tee if it isn't your honour *(right)*.

Do keep an eye on the group in front. If they stretch out a gap of say one hole, make every effort to catch up.

Do make sure you are ready to play when it's your turn. If it's an approach shot to a green, make your club selection calculations and practice swings while your playing partner or fellow competitors are hitting their shots. As long as you're not in their line of sight, you won't put them off. On the green, you can easily find a few seconds to read the line of a putt while others are themselves preparing to putt.

Finally, remember it isn't about whether you win or lose but how you play the game, so always smile and shake hands afterward.

The rules of play

The game itself

Golf has always consisted of playing a ball from the teeing ground into the hole by a stroke, or successive strokes, in accordance with the rules of the game. It sounds a simple enough pursuit and certainly the definition gives few clues as to the challenges, which are among the attractions of the game. Another appealing aspect is the number of different formats in which the game can be played. For everyday play, there are two main formats.

Matchplay

This is thought to have been the original form of golf and is, in fact, the main format of play at some of the older established clubs.

Above: Head-to-head matchplay is the original and, some still say, the best form of golf. Always shake hands and wish your opponent well.

The terms of engagement are straightforward enough. The game is played by holes. A hole is won by the side, or player, that takes the fewest strokes on each given hole. So if you win the first hole, you are then what is described as 'one up.' If you lose the first hole, you are 'one down' and if you halve it, in other words take the same number of shots as your opponent, you are 'all square.' Each subsequent hole is played on the same basis, the score being kept on a cumulative basis.

The outcome of the game is decided when you are either 'up' or 'down' by more holes than there are left to play. So, for instance, in a match played over one round, if you reach a situation where you are 'four up' with only three holes to play you are deemed to have won the match by the margin of 4&3. Conversely, say you lose the 17th to go two down with only the final hole to play, you are the loser, this time by a margin of 2&1.

'Dormie' is a term used to describe a situation where you or your opponent are 'down' by the same number of holes that are left to play. So let's say you are having a good day and you've just won the 15th to go 'three up', your opponent is thus 'dormie-three down.'

If a competition dictates that a result must be achieved, then in the event of a tie after 18 holes a sudden-death playoff normally ensues. Players simply proceed again to the first tee. The match is decided when a player or side wins a hole.

One of the nuances of matchplay that separates it from other forms of play is the 'concession,' whereby your opponent is allowed to concede you a putt from short range. Equally, if you are feeling generous, you too can concede putts to your opponent. It's a charming aspect of the game and, as well as saving time, has an element of gamesmanship to it. For instance, early in a round, when there's no pressure, you may decide to concede your opponent a two-footer, perhaps lulling him into the feeling that all putts of that length will be conceded. Then, later in the

Pro Tip

Change the order of play in fourball betterball

One of the major strategic benefits in fourball betterball is the fact you can swap the honour with your partner at any time. So on the tee the player teeing off first can get the ball safely in play, giving his partner the opportunity to attack.

Equally, you can mix up the order of play on the greens. The rules suggest that the player furthest from the hole putts first, but in a fourball match you are allowed to switch the order to your advantage. You will actually see this happen quite a lot in Ryder Cup matches and it can be an effective tactic. Let's say you have a 25ft (7.6m) putt for birdie and your partner has a four-footer for par. Providing your partner is pretty confident of holing out, it might be wise for him to putt first. With a par safely secured you have a 'free putt' – in other words, you can give it a good run at the hole without worrying about having to hole the return putt. Playing with that peace of mind can only improve your chances of holing the birdie putt.

PROBLEM SOLVER

My friend and I were drawn against one another in an important matchplay knockout competition. To save any awkward or embarrassing moments on the greens, we came to an agreement whereby every putt inside the length of the putter-grip would be conceded. Someone in the clubhouse heard us discussing this and suggested it was not allowed. Was he right?

In a word, yes. Strokes cannot be conceded in advance. The rules of golf categorically state that the only stroke which may be conceded is 'the next stroke.' Therefore you could both have been disqualified if you had gone ahead with such an agreement.

round, you can surprise him by making him hole an 18-inch (45cm) putt, when the pressure is on. Of course, you may have the same done to you, but that's one of the many 'attractions' of match play.

Strokeplay

This form of golf now dominates competitive play at clubs around the world. It's all about you, your clubs, a pencil and a score card. It's the format the professionals play by on tour 99 percent of the time and it's the format you will face in club medals.

The principle couldn't be simpler. Each competitor compiles a score and the winner is the one with the lowest total. The outcome is based either on the net score – in other words, the total number of strokes minus the player's handicap – or gross score, where no handicaps are taken into account. The latter is the way the pros play, obviously, and that's how leading tournaments such as club championship are decided in the amateur game.

Unlike matchplay, no one can grant you a concession in strokeplay, so don't expect compassion from your playing partner when you rattle a putt 3ft (0.9m) past the hole and don't like the prospect of the putt coming back. He can't help you. Nobody can. You're on your own and, like it or not, you have to hole out on every green.

Above: It is each and every golfer's responsibility to keep score in a strokeplay competition.

Keep score, but try to lose count

In the interests of accuracy it's best for you to mark a scorecard after every hole, otherwise you can easily make mistakes. But saying that, it's a good idea to get yourself into the habit of mentally forgetting what your running total is. That way you can more easily focus on one shot, and one hole, at a time.

If, on the other hand, you are constantly mindful of your score relative to par or your handicap, there's a danger you start to plan ahead. 'If I can just par the last three holes,' goes the usual logic 'I'll beat my best ever score and maybe even win the competition.' That's just tempting fate. Stay in the present and avoid predictions and plans. You'll be far more successful at strokeplay if you can train yourself to do that.

Pro Tip

Other forms of play

Whereas most pursuits exist in one particular format, golf is completely the opposite. There are dozens of different ways to keep score and compete against an opponent, each fascinating in its own way. Some of these games will actually form the basis of official competitions at certain clubs. Others are really only to be enjoyed among a group of friends. Whatever the reason, all the variations are worth a try.

Foursomes

A popular game at many clubs, this format involves two teams of two playing against one another over 18 holes. Much quicker than the everyday game, it is often played in winter, when a brisk pace of play is desirable.

Each pair plays the same ball, with one partner teeing off on the odd-numbered holes and the other partner teeing off on the even-numbered holes. Once the tee shots are hit, the pair play alternate shots until the ball is either holed or conceded by the opponents. Because each player knows that it is their partner's responsibility to play the next shot, foursomes involves a strong element of teamwork and camaraderie.

Also, there is a certain amount of strategy involved in deciding who tees off at the odds or evens. The longer hitter of the two is obviously best utilised on the long holes, so a team

Above: In foursomes partners play alternate shots until the ball is holed, or a putt is conceded.

would try to avoid having him or her hitting too many tee shots on par-3s. Likewise, an accurate, but short, hitter doesn't want to be on the tee on the longest holes on the course. Neither would you want a great pitcher of the ball playing too many tee shots on short par-4s, when his strengths lie in hitting accurate approach shots.

Shots are given or received on the basis of three-eighths of the difference of the combined handicaps of each pair. So, for instance, if team A has a combined handicap of 23 and team B has a combined handicap of 7, then team A will receive six shots over 18 holes (in other words, three-eighths of the combined difference of 16).

Stableford

This is a popular form of scoring at golf clubs around the world and can be applied to a variety of different playing formats; singles, fourball betterball, foursomes, greensomes, almost any game in fact. The key factor is that it's a pencil-and-score-card system, although very different from normal medal play.

Basically, the number of shots you take on each hole earns a certain number of points. A par is worth two points, a bogey is one point, a birdie three points, an eagle four points and that rarest of birds, an albatross, five points. If you can't score better than a bogey you pick your ball up and score no points for that hole. You then add up all of these points at the end of the round and the highest score wins.

Naturally, handicaps come into play in most stableford competitions and that means that your net score is the one that counts. The number of strokes received is usually calculated on three-quarters of your full handicap. So if you play off a handicap of 16, you will receive a stroke on every hole with a stroke index on the card of 12 and under. So on stroke index number five, your par is effectively a birdie, your bogey effectively a par, and so on. It's a great format, not least because your total disaster holes count no worse than a double-bogey; on a par-4 you can take 10 shots or seven, the result is still the same, *nil points*.

Greensomes

This is a more forgiving, and frequently played, variation of foursomes. It involves a partnership hitting alternate shots with the same ball, but only after both players have teed off and chosen the best drive. There's no decision-making required on the odds and evens. Both players drive off and then decide on the most favourably positioned of the two balls, from which to play alternate shots.

Greensomes is really popular at society and guest invitation days and has almost replaced foursomes at these events. For one thing, it feels more of a complete round because both players get to tee off on every one of the 18 holes, and if you are only playing that particular course, say, once a year then that's obviously desirable. Also, it's not as mentally demanding as foursomes. Each pairing has at least two opportunities to get a good tee shot away on each hole, whereas with foursomes that responsibility falls to one player.

Yellowsomes

This is a cruel variation of greensomes and, make no mistake, there is potential here for disaster on a grand scale. It must be said, though, that it can be great fun when played in the right company, ideally friends. The concept is identical to greensomes. Played on a two-against-two basis, both golfers in each pairing tee off on every hole, then hit alternate shots from then on. The difference is that instead of each pair selecting their best tee shot, as with greensomes, in yellowsomes it is the opponents who get to pick the worst tee shot of the two. If you and your partner both hit the fairway, count your blessings because you are guaranteed a shot from the short grass. If you hit a great drive, though, and your partner doesn't, well ... you're not going to like your next shot, that's for sure. There's even more pressure in this game than in regular foursomes, because the last thing you want to do is land your partner in trouble after he's just nailed one down the middle of the fairway.

Texas Scramble

This is another popular format on guest invitation days. Texas Scramble can be played in teams of two, three or four, although the principle remains the same irrespective of the number of players in each team. Each member of the team tees off and they then decide on the best drive. Every member of the team then hits a second shot from that spot. The best-placed second shot is then chosen and again every member of the team plays a third shot from that spot. So every member of the team has a go at the same drive, the same second shot, the same putt and so on until someone holes out.

As you can imagine it is possible to shoot some amazingly low scores; in a group of useful amateurs an under-par score in the teens is quite commonplace. It's a huge thrill to be racking-up birdies like never before, and from a social standpoint it's an unbeatable format because players in a team hardly ever leave each other's side. If there is a downside to Texas Scramble it is that it can take rather a long time to get around the 18 holes.

American Stableford

This is often known by the numerical tag '6-3-0' and that provides a strong clue as to the nature of this scoring format.

It's the perfect game when you are in a threeball, either out of choice or perhaps due to the fourth member of a fourball group oversleeping! There are a possible nine points up for grabs on every hole. Six points for the player who wins the hole outright, three for the player who secures second place, and no points for the player who finishes last. Points are accumulated on this basis through the course of the round. If there's a two-way tie for the lowest score on a particular hole, the points are distributed 3-3-0. If there's a three-way tie then obviously the score remains unchanged. The player with the highest number of points after 18 holes is the winner. The handicap allowance is identical to regular match play: three-quarters of the difference.

Cross Country

A rare game these days, as greenskeepers become increasingly sensitive to the damaging effect it can have on the course.

The name gives away the nature of the game, really. The self-appointed architects of the tournament literally throw away the score card and come up with a series of 'new' one-off holes, usually nine, that bear absolutely no resemblance to the existing pattern of holes on the course. So you might play from the 1st tee to the 5th green, or from the 9th tee to the 8th green, or whatever other bizarre creation happens to come to the new course architect's mind. It's challenging, interesting and, above all, great fun.

The tools of the trade

Much deliberation goes into choosing golf equipment, and rightly so, because it isn't cheap. But do you know what you are and are not allowed to carry in your golf bag? You should, because ignorance is no excuse if you break the rules.

Rule 4 | Clubs

There was a time when there was no limit to the number of clubs you were allowed to carry on to the golf course. While caddies may not have relished the prospect of bearing such a burden, the players would surely have delighted at the freedom of choice. No limit on numbers meant a profusion of specialist, or 'utility' clubs, with hardly a situation that a player couldn't prepare for in the shape of a club designed specifically for the job.

All good things come to an end, though, and the authorities eventually decided that the situation needed regulating. In the 1930s a limit of 14 clubs was imposed by the governing bodies of golf... and caddies all round the world rejoiced! The figure has remained at this level ever since.

The rules relating to clubs, however, are broader than simply limiting the number of 'sticks' a golfer can carry.

Above: The maximum number of clubs allowed is 14. Penalties apply if a golfer exceeds this quota.

If you break a club

There are many ways of breaking a club, apart from in anger. If you break a club in the normal course of play, then you are perfectly entitled to replace it with another, providing you can do so without delaying play.

If, however, you do break a club in anger, that's tough. You can't replace it, you just have to live with it and hope it isn't a crucial one, such as a putter or driver. The US tour pro Ben Crenshaw managed to snap the shaft of his putter during the back nine in a Ryder Cup singles match at Muirfield Village in 1987 and had to putt with a 2-iron on the remaining greens – not something which helped his cause. Not even his magical talent on the greens could spare him from defeat at the hands of Irishman Eamon Darcy, who's slippery-quick putt on the final green actually secured the Cup for the European team.

If you want to add to your set

This, in some ways, is one of the most lenient rules in the book. If you are in the middle of a round and you decide, for whatever reason, that you want to add a club to your existing set, then you are perfectly entitled to do so. Again, it's on the proviso that you don't hold up play and, of course, providing you don't already have 14 clubs in your bag.

Above: It is always prudent to check the number of clubs in your bag, prior to making your way to the first tee.

If you carry too many clubs

This breach of the rule book can have serious consequences, so always check the number of clubs before you go out. The penalty for a breach of this rule depends on whether you are involved in a matchplay or strokeplay event.

If it's matchplay, the penalty depends how far you are into the game, because you basically have to deduct one hole for every hole you've carried the extra baggage, up to a maximum of two holes. So if you've played four holes and suddenly come across a 15th club in your bag, you are two down before you've even taken into account the actual match score.

Pro Tip

Keep your grooves clean

It's surprising the state some amateurs let their clubs get into, the most common and costly oversight being grooves on the clubface clogged up with mud. It's important you understand that the grooves must be clean in order for you to be able to generate backspin on an iron shot, which is essential for the proper trajectory and check-spin on landing. This is especially true with the short irons, where you are looking for maximum control. You won't get that if your clubs are dirty, so in between shots scrape out any mud from the grooves with a wooden tee-peg. It takes no time at all, but makes a significant difference to your shots.

In a strokeplay event, you are penalised two strokes for each hole played with that extra 'baggage,' this time up to a maximum of four strokes. That's just as costly as the match play penalty, because if you don't discover your mistake until the third, you have to add four strokes to your score at the end of the round. That's like playing one more hole than everyone else – very costly!

Incidentally, it doesn't matter if you are carrying one extra club or five, the penalty is the same. Somewhat surprisingly, you can also share clubs, provided the total number of clubs shared between you is no more than 14.

PROBLEM SOLVER

I was playing in a competition recently and on one tee, just as I got to the top of my backswing, the chap I was playing with dropped his club on the ground. Not surprisingly it distracted me and I hit a terrible shot into the trees. Is there any ruling which allows me to replay the shot?
Sadly, no. It seems harsh, but distractions are considered part and parcel of the game and therefore all players must accept the consequences.

Rule 5 | The ball

You may take the ball for granted, but that little white thing is a complicated piece of equipment. For a start, its dimensions and performance characteristics are rigidly monitored by the game's governing bodies. The ball must not be designed, manufactured or intentionally modified to have flight properties different from those of a symmetrically spherical ball. It must be not less than 1.68in (4.26cm) in diameter, although there are larger golf balls on the market, and it must not weigh more than 1.62oz (45gr). Nor should its initial velocity be permitted to exceed 250fps (76mps). And, just so you know, no foreign material may be applied to the ball for the purposes of changing its playing characteristics.

Above: If a golfer feels that a ball is damaged, confirmation must be sought from a fellow competitor or opponent.

Damaged goods

The rules are very specific about what constitutes 'damage' on a golf ball and the appropriate procedures must be followed to the letter. Basically, a ball is described as 'unfit for play' when it is visibly cut, cracked or out of shape. If you have reason to believe that your ball is damaged in some way – perhaps you have just thinned an iron shot and think it might have put a 'smile' on the ball – then you are entitled to pick it up to inspect it. However, you must first notify your fellow competitors of your intentions and, in the presence of a witness, mark its position with, say, a tee-peg or coin. Now you can pick it up and it is up to your fellow competitor to verify the decision. If there is a consensus that the ball is indeed damaged, then you can go ahead and replace it before you play your next shot.

The procedure is the key here. You must call over your fellow competitor before you even touch the ball. Failure to comply with this 'ID Protocol' carries a one-shot penalty in a strokeplay event and an immediate loss of hole in matchplay.

Breaking-up is hard to do

It isn't likely to happen very often, but let's just say the ball you are playing does break into pieces at the moment of impact. It will certainly come as a bit of a shock, but what happens next? Well, the rules are naturally sympathetic. It's clearly not your fault, so before you compose your letter of complaint to the manufacturer, simply cancel that stroke and play another ball from the same spot. There's no penalty involved.

Personal ID

As anyone who has ever been in a golf shop will have noticed, there are an awful lot of different balls on the market. On top of that, golf balls are numbered, typically from one to eight. Together then, this creates a series of permutations that run into the thousands. Surely, therefore, you are unlikely to confuse two golf balls on the course? Don't you believe it. Identical golf balls can come into close contact on the course and that's a recipe not only for confusion, but disaster.

Surprisingly there have been many cases of mistaken identity in professional tournaments down through the years. The former Ryder Cup player, captain, and teaching guru John Jacobs recalls one such incident when he was competing in the French Open Championship in the 1950s.

Above: It's wise to personalise your golf ball to avoid any problems with identification.

Use a ball that fits in with your priorities

Golf balls are expensive these days, but try to avoid playing with any old ball that you find in the trees or in the rough at your home club. Decide what your priorities are in the game, distance or control, and select a ball that suits your strategy. Your pro will be happy to advise you on this subject, should you be confused by the number of different makes on the shelf. Then try to stick with that choice so you can develop a familiarity with the ball's playing characteristics. Your game is bound to benefit from the continuity of using the same type of ball, especially on and around the greens where touch and feel is such an important issue.

Jacobs's good friend Harold Henning was in a share for second place playing the 17th hole, where his drive ran into the rough where there were lots of fallen leaves. He found a ball the same make as his own, a Slazenger B51, and it was the same number as well. Perhaps understandably assuming it was his, he played an iron shot to the green, putted out, and only when he retrieved the ball from the hole did he realise it was not in fact his ball. Immediately he disqualified himself.

Such is the spirit and camaraderie that exists in the game of golf, his fellow professionals had a whip-round on the bus to the airport and handed the money to an emotional Henning. The sum amounted to roughly the equivalent of a second-place finish. A painful episode... with a happy ending!

So, this is why it is always wise to personalise your golf balls. It's easy enough to do, by simply making a 'mark' of your own, such as a pattern of dots or a squiggle around the maker's name, with a permanent marker.

If you consider this unnecessary, think again. Virtually every tour pro does it. There is a documented incident in a club competition of two golfers each looking for their golf ball in the same patch of rough. They found both balls, sitting virtually side by side. But the manufacturer's name was the same... and so was the number. Of course, neither golfer could identify which ball was his. So what was the ruling? Both were deemed 'lost balls.' Learning the Rules of Golf can sometimes be a painful experience.

Rule 6 | The player

You may think that trying to put together a good competition round is more than enough to worry about on the course, but alas there are other responsibilities that fall on your shoulders. To be honest, they're not especially onerous, but if you're not clued-up it is easy to miss something and end up paying the penalty.

Handicap

It's up to you to know your playing handicap. In matchplay, it is this information that determines the number of strokes given or received. If you start a match having declared an incorrect handicap, even if by mistake, this obviously affects the number of strokes given and you are disqualified.

The penalty is equally harsh if you make the same mistake in a strokeplay event. It's up to you to know your handicap and to record this information on the score card before you sign and return it. If you fail to do so, or you enter the wrong handicap, which naturally affects the number of strokes you receive, then once again you are disqualified from the competition.

Be punctual

Starting times in competitions are there for a reason and you have to adhere to them or face disqualification. There is, however, the merest hint of leniency with this rule. If you arrive at the first tee within five minutes of your allotted starting time and are ready and able to tee off, then the committee may waive the penalty of disqualification and simply impose a two-shot penalty in strokeplay or loss of the first hole in matchplay. Don't bank on this, though, as you must have a very good excuse. Also, any reprieve assumes you can find a member of the committee at that exact moment in time (unlikely!) or the club pro or secretary of the club, who fulfil the same role in the absence of a committee member.

Learn to keep count

Within this ruling lurks another potential nightmare, because submitting a score card with an incorrect score on a hole is a no-win

Watch the line all the way

If ever you miss a putt, it's always preferable to miss it past the hole. Why? For one thing the ball will never go in if you leave it short. Also, you can watch what the ball does in its journey beyond the hole *(below)*, which helps give you the correct line for the return putt. That's why you should never turn away in disgust if your ball misses. Watch it all the way. It'll make your next putt that much easier.

situation. If your card records a score on any hole that is higher than the number of strokes you actually took, then that higher score stands. If, on the other hand, your score card states a score on any hole that is lower than the number of strokes you took, then you are disqualified.

This may seem harsh bearing in mind that it is your fellow competitor, not you, who marks your card. The onus, however, is on you to check it thoroughly before you sign it. Don't take anything for granted. You only have to look back to the 1968 US Masters for a heartbreaking example of this very strict rule. Roberto de Vicenzo completed his final round level with Bob Goalby and was no doubt mentally prepared to compete in the playoff that would decide the championship. To his horror, however, minutes later he discovered that his playing partner had marked him down for a four on the penultimate hole instead of the three he had actually taken. De Vicenzo hadn't spotted the mistake, had thus signed his card and the higher score counted. This meant that he was one stroke behind and Bob Goalby was declared the winner.

Looking on the bright side, especially for the mathematically challenged, no one is penalised for incorrect addition. If the individual scores for each hole are entered correctly, but you add them up incorrectly, you are in the clear because it's up to the committee to ensure that all the numbers add up.

Stop and go

A round of golf on the professional tour has become a painfully slow experience, sometimes as long as four-and-a-half, or even five, hours for a threeball. But perhaps the most worrying aspect of this is that 'slow-play syndrome' appears to have spread to the amateur game.

Don't succumb to the snail's pace. It makes life miserable for everyone and you may one day get penalised for it. Indeed, it's a two-stroke penalty in strokeplay and the loss of a hole in matchplay if you continually hold up play. If you then don't get a move on you may even be disqualified altogether.

YES, torrential rain is incredibly unpleasant, makes your grips slip and your feet sodden. But **NO**, you can't use it as an excuse to stop playing. **YES**, if the course becomes unplayable through flooding you can then stop and **YES**, lightning is a good enough excuse – the rules do allow you to stop if you feel you are in danger.

PROBLEM SOLVER

I was involved in a match in which we discovered after the round was completed that a stroke had been given on the wrong hole. Does this have an effect on the final result?
No, since this was obviously a genuine mistake and there was no attempt by either party to gain any form of advantage, the result should stand as it is.

Rule 7 Practice

There are obviously no rules of golf applicable when you're at the driving range or hitting balls on the practice green – apart from the various safety considerations, of course – so this particular aspect of the rule book outlines to what extent you are permitted to practise on the course during a competitive round. It is a delicate subject and you need to be absolutely clear on it and adhere religiously to the correct procedures otherwise you will incur penalties.

Let's first deal with strokeplay, the strictest of the two formats. Most crucially of all, you are not allowed to practise on the golf course before your round. Neither can you practise on the course between rounds in a 36-hole competition, even if the rounds are to be played on consecutive days. This means that from the moment you finish your first round on Saturday lunch time, say, you can't decide to go out on the course to

Left: Warming up before a round is good for your game, but be aware that certain rules exist which, if breached, are not good for your score.

hit a few balls prior to your second round on Sunday. If you are caught doing this – even if it's something as apparently harmless as hitting a putt on one of the greens – you will be disqualified.

In matchplay, however, you can practise on the golf course before your round. Once you are on the course, either in matchplay or strokeplay, the rules do allow you some leeway on practising. For instance, after holing out on a green, you are allowed to practice putt or chip on or around the green of the hole you have just finished playing. You cannot hit a practice shot out of a hazard, though, such as a bunker. Neither can you practise on the green if it means that you unduly delay play – remember, a golfer who unduly delays play is himself subject to penalty. The penalty for any breach of this rule is two strokes in a strokeplay event and the loss of hole in matchplay. An interesting point here is that the loss of hole in matchplay applies to the next hole, rather than the hole you've just played. So if one of you in a match breaches the rule by playing out of a bunker, say on the 5th green after you've both holed out, you can basically skip the 6th hole because the offender will have forfeited that hole without even getting to the tee.

Don't take practising on the golf course lightly. Even casually knocking a stray ball back on to the range can land you in trouble if it is felt that in doing so you might have been working on, say, the rhythm of your swing. It sounds ridiculous, but you can get pulled-up in an instant on any one of these points, so it really is important you think before you act. Just one moment of impetuosity can cost you very dearly.

PROBLEM SOLVER

I was having a debate recently with a friend who was arguing that it is quite permissible to send a caddie out on to the course prior to a competition in order to test the speed of the greens, identify where the subtle breaks are, and so on. Surely this is a breach of the Rules?

*No, actually it isn't. The Rules state that a player is responsible for the actions of his caddie **only during the round itself**. Your friend has hit on a good idea... if he can persuade his caddie to prepare in such thorough fashion, that is!*

Pro Tip

Chips and putts get you tuned in for the game

Most of you have probably neither the time nor the inclination to put in a lot of practice before you go out. At best you might have 10–15 minutes between changing into your shoes and stepping on the first tee. That doesn't mean to say you can't put in some valuable pre-round practice, though. Even a little is better than nothing.

When time is short, it's best to restrict yourself to chips and putts. Take your favourite chipping club and half-a-dozen balls and hit some different length chip shots to a variety of targets on the practice green. This gets your mind in tune with the game and quickly develops your feel. If the club doesn't allow chipping on to the practice putting green, which is not uncommon, simply chip to a few makeshift targets to the side. The benefits are virtually the same.

When you practise your putting, don't sweat over lots of 3- and 4-footers. You might miss more than you make, which does you no good at all. Instead, stroke a few long putts across the green and try to develop your feel for distance. Hit a few short putts if you wish, but try to restrict yourself to a range where you get used to seeing the ball hit the back of the hole, rather than slipping past.

Right: Chipping practice is a great way to get tuned-in for an upcoming game.

Rule 8 | Advice

Remember from the definitions earlier in the book, advice is described as 'any counsel or suggestion which could influence a player in determining his play, the choice of club, or the method of making a stroke.'

Basically, this means that you can ask questions on matters that are described as 'public information,' such as what distance it is from, say, a certain tree or fixed sprinkler head to the front of the green. The key point is that these are permanent objects. Therefore, the interpretation is such that no golfer is gaining an advantage – unfair or otherwise – from information on their whereabouts.

However, you can't ask that same person what the distance is from your golf ball to the front of the green. It may seem like splitting hairs, but it's important you understand this subtle distinction, because Murphy's Law states that the one time you do phrase the question incorrectly it will be directed at the canny rules expert who is always looking for a sniff of an advantage – no matter how underhand it might seem. And, of course, there's always a chance that someone will overhear you. So even if the person you ask doesn't have a problem with it, another golfer just might.

There are many other examples of the nuances of what constitutes advice and what doesn't. It pays to make a mental note of these.

You **cannot** ask your opponent or fellow competitor what club they have just hit.

You **can**, however, peer into his or her golf bag to see the number on the club. If, understandably, that person doesn't want you to know and covers his clubs with a towel, for instance, you **cannot** fling the towel away to catch a sneaky glimpse.

You **cannot** give technical advice to your opponent or fellow competitor. OK, so you probably won't want to tell an opponent where he's going wrong at the top of his backswing, but even if you're five-up in a matchplay game and suddenly overcome by goodwill, you must resist the temptation because it is you who will be penalised for giving the advice in this instance. Your opponent cannot be penalised for hearing something and will be delighted to win a hole back unexpectedly. If in doubt, say nothing!

Above: Don't be too influenced in your club selection by the actions of others.

Pro Tip

Play your own game

As we've already discussed in this section on advice, it might occasionally be tempting to want to see what club your fellow competitor has hit, say into a par-3, but it's potentially dangerous to be swayed by the actions of others. If you already have an idea in your own mind about what club you are going to hit, that first instinct is usually the correct one and it's nearly always best to stick with that. Besides, you have no idea how purely your fellow competitor struck the ball or for that matter whether they eased up on it or gave it a little extra. So looking to see what club was in their hands doesn't necessarily help you. In fact, it might even mislead you and cause you to misjudge your shot.

Pro Tip

Give yourself a line...

As we've made quite clear, having the line of a putt indicated to you is a delicate area. You can't have any marks put down on the green, nor can your caddie stand in such a way as to give you something to aim at. However, one technique that a lot of tour players use in helping them hit putts on their chosen line is placing the ball in such a way that the manufacturer's mark runs parallel with the line of the putt *(right)*. This gives you an extra visual aid in lining up the putter and makes it easier to start the ball rolling on the correct line. Why not give it a try.

...or treat every putt as straight

Not as confusing as it sounds, this one. Again, this is a tactic used by many of the world's best players. Once the putt is read and the exact amount of break determined, some players will, to all intents and purposes, ignore the actual hole location. Instead they will focus on a spot to the side of the hole, which is equivalent to the amount of break on that putt. Then all that is required is a straight putt at this imaginary target. Simple. Of course, there are sometimes imperfections in the putting surface which can be used as a target. Many golfers find that treating every putt as straight, in this way, leads to a better stroke. Why not give it a try?

Indicating the line of play

You will recall the definition relating to 'line of play.' It is the 'direction that the player wishes his ball to take, plus a reasonable distance either side of that line.' Understandably you need to be careful about this line of play, especially when you are on the green. It is a sensitive area.

When you are preparing to putt, the line of play may be pointed out to you, say, by your caddie, but in doing so the line of play must not be touched and the caddie must move away before you begin your stroke. Neither can a mark be put down to indicate the line for putting.

Away from the putting green things become a little more relaxed. Basically, if you can't see what you're aiming at, anyone can help you by indicating the line to the target. However, that person must move before you play the stroke, which they may wish to do anyway in the interests of safety! But if it is a particularly brave individual, or a very loyal friend, just make sure they move in the interests of your score! It's a two-stroke penalty for that breach of the rules, or loss of hole in match play.

Rule 9 Information

All parties involved in a match should be aware of the number of strokes taken, including any penalty strokes incurred along the way. So if you incur a penalty you have to inform either your fellow competitor or your opponent as soon as is practicable. Failure to do so is like being asked how many you took on a given hole and coming up with the wrong answer – and that's cheating!

Bear in mind that you don't have to state the obvious. If you are playing a par-3 over water and your tee shot plummets into the drink 50yds (45m) short of the green, words are perhaps neither necessary nor desirable – from either party!

PROBLEM SOLVER

In a recent round of our club championship knockout, I lost a hole to an opponent who discovered on the next tee that he had played the wrong ball on that hole? Presumably, I could have claimed the hole?

Yes, that's correct. It was obviously a genuine mistake on your opponent's behalf; nevertheless, he effectively gave you wrong information as to the number of strokes taken on that hole. Therefore, you won that hole.

The order of play

It would be mayhem on the golf course, with balls flying from all directions, if there was no distinct rule governing the actual order of play. Imagine it; in a group of four it would be hard to figure out what on earth was going on. Not only that, it would be quite dangerous. So, here are the order of play procedures that help keep things running smoothly from the first tee to the final green.

Rule 10 The order of play

On the tee

The side, or player, entitled to tee off first is said to have the 'honour.' This is decided on the first tee either by the order of the starting sheet, perhaps by order of handicap (lowest first) or in matchplay by whichever name is highest on the draw sheet. In the absence of this information it can simply be decided on the toss of a coin.

Above: Honour on the first tee is often determined by handicap order, especially in competition play; other times, more simply, by the toss of a coin.

Thereafter it could not be simpler. The golfer or side with the lowest score on each hole takes the honour on the next tee. It is decided on the gross score in a strokeplay event and on the net score – in other words, with strokes taken into account – in a matchplay competition. If a hole is halved, then the honour is simply retained by the golfer who teed-off first on the previous hole.

Losing order

Strictly speaking, playing out of turn off the tee in a strokeplay event carries no penalty. But you shouldn't make a habit of it. For one thing it is considered very poor etiquette and could really aggravate your fellow competitors. Worse still, if a committee decides that an unfair advantage is being sought in doing so – for all they know competitors may have cooked up some mutual arrangement – then those golfers can be disqualified from the competition.

The rules are different in matchplay, though. If you tee off when it isn't your turn, your opponent is entitled to cancel that shot and ask you to play it again. Much depends on the quality of the shot. Obviously he or she wouldn't exercise that option if you had just knocked your ball into a fairway bunker – the opponent is equally entitled to let the shot stand – but if you've just hit your finest drive down the middle of the fairway you may, in some company, find yourself re-teeing a second ball. And you won't relish that prospect.

Provisional ball

If you need to play a provisional ball or a second ball from the tee – perhaps having struck a ball out of bounds – you should do so after your opponent or fellow competitors have hit their first tee shots. That is the correct order of play. Also, it has merit in the sense that it's good to gather your thoughts and compose yourself after a destructive shot, rather than rush in impulsively and hit another ball.

Elsewhere on the course

Once you're off the tee, the order of play is determined by distance from the flag and it is the golfer furthest from the hole who is entitled to play first. There is no penalty for playing out of order in strokeplay, although once again it is worth stressing that such behaviour is very bad etiquette. But in matchplay an opponent can cancel the stroke and request that it be played again.

Putting out

The green is the one area of the course where the order of play is not necessarily determined by who is furthest from the hole. First putts are usually determined by that, but when the balls get closer to the hole, the order of play can change.

For instance, in strokeplay you can carry on putting until the ball is in the hole, although it is good etiquette to ensure that you don't trample all

Above: The order of play on the green is not always decided by who is farthest from the hole.

PROBLEM SOLVER

What happens when two balls are so far apart that it is almost impossible to determine who should play first?
In such situations, the order of play should simply be determined by lot. That is the only sensible and convenient solution. It only requires a toss of a coin to help avoid any arguments.

Pro Tip

Practice stroke accidents

Here's a funny situation, the ball being struck with the toe-end of the putter during a practice putting stroke *(right)*. Actually, it might look funny to the onlooker, but it's no laughing matter for the perpetrator who unfortunately must accept a one-stroke penalty for moving a ball that is in play. The ball must then be replaced before continuing. The moral of the story? Stand well away from the ball when you make your practice putting strokes. It's better to be safe than sorry.

Strangely enough, there is no penalty if you commit the same offence on the tee – in other words, clip the ball while making a practice swing. This is because when on the tee the ball is effectively not yet in play. In that situation you simply put it back on the tee-peg and start again.

over someone else's line to the hole. In matchplay, however, you do not have that right. You can, of course, ask your opponent if you can hole out, but your request will almost certainly be declined.

Measuring distance

On the green it can often be difficult to tell whose ball is furthest from the hole and thus who should putt first. This is where you need to do a bit of measuring, either with the flagstick or by pacing it out. If by accident you move the ball in the process of measuring distance, there is no penalty. You simply replace it on its original spot.

The teeing ground

This is where it all starts – possibly the beginning of a new round and, at the very least, the beginning of a new hole. Make no mistake, a good start comes down to more than simply producing a fine golf swing.

Rule 11 | The teeing ground

The teeing ground, or tee-box, is a rectangular area two club-lengths deep bordered either side by two tee-markers. You cannot move either of the two tee-markers, but you can stand outside them provided the ball is teed between them.

There are more benefits to this than you might imagine. Utilising the full width of the teeing ground can improve your 'angle of attack on certain holes, perhaps giving you a more direct line into a cunningly positioned flag on a par-3.

Above: The depth of the teeing ground is two club-lengths, should you so wish to make the most of this space.

Using the full two club-lengths depth of the teeing ground can also prove beneficial, particularly in the winter months, when the soft ground might be in poor condition as a result of lots of golfers trampling around in the same area. Just stepping back a

Above: You may stand outside either of the two tee markers, providing the ball is teed within them.

Above: If trouble is on the right-hand side, tee up on the right and aim away from it.

Pro Tip

Aim away from the trouble

Here's a simple strategy which helps you stay out of trouble when hazards or trees lurk on one side of the fairway. Let's say, for instance, you have a hole at your regular club where there is a heavily wooded area down the right-hand side of the fairway. This creates something of a mental block and you typically really struggle to find the fairway. Well, if you tee your ball on the extreme right-hand side of the teeing ground, you can aim down the left side of the fairway and, in effect, shoot away from the trouble down the right. This gives you a significantly greater margin for error; you basically have the entire width of the fairway to play with.

And think of the alternative; if you tee up equidistant between the two tee-markers and aim straight down the middle, you've got only half the width of the fairway to play with. Mentally, that can make all the difference between making a confident swing as opposed to a tentative hit-and-hope.

couple of club-lengths from the target may afford you the opportunity of teeing off on turf which is far less worn, perhaps even quite pristine. That's sure to give you a more secure footing and will thus help you play a better shot, too.

Here are a few reminders to make sure you don't incur penalties on the teeing ground.

False start

Let's dispel a common myth...and, at the same time, a very lame joke! If at address you nudge the ball off its tee-peg with your clubhead, ignore the smart-aleck who says 'one.' For a start, that accidental nudge does not constitute one shot – you simply replace the ball on the tee and start again. And secondly, as we've said, it's a truly feeble attempt at humour, so don't even feel you need to offer a reply.

Out of place

If by mistake you play a shot from outside the teeing ground, the rules vary according to the format of the game you're playing and, to a certain degree, the benevolence of your opponent.

In matchplay your opponent has every right to ask you to play the shot again, admittedly without penalty, but again it all depends on the type of shot you've just hit. If you've just smashed your ball straight down the middle, there's every chance you may find yourself 'reloading' and hitting another drive. So, no penalty as such. But it will feel like a 'mental penalty,' especially if your second attempt doesn't quite match the quality of the first.

In strokeplay the procedures are more clear cut. If you play a shot from outside the tee markers you incur a penalty of two strokes and then have to play a ball from between the tee-markers. This is then called 'three off the tee'.

Incidentally, even if you mistakenly play from the back tee, when there is obviously no advantage gained because you are effectively playing a longer hole than everyone else, you are still in breach of the rules and the procedures outlined above therefore apply.

Pro Tip

Always stick to your routine

A pre-shot routine helps focus your mind on the job at hand and promotes consistency, both in the set-up and the swing. If your normal routine is interrupted in some way, say as a result of accidentally nudging the ball off its tee-peg, compose yourself and start again. Put the ball back on the tee-peg and proceed as if the incident had never happened – in other words, from the beginning again. That way you'll regain your focus and be better able to concentrate on the shot.

Left: All good golfers have a pre-shot routine, which gets them mentally 'into' the shot.

PROBLEM SOLVER

A friend of mine who is a total novice when it comes to golf took a swipe at a ball from the tee and barely clipped it, and the ball didn't even get off the teeing ground. He then claimed he could tee up the ball again, on the basis that he was still on the tee. It had a weird kind of logic, but it didn't seem right. What is the ruling?

Your friend was sadly in the wrong. That first shot, though admittedly feeble, was a genuine stroke and therefore the ball was then officially 'in play.'

Playing the ball

This is the whole essence of the game – hitting that little white, spherical object. Not only is it a complicated process from a physical standpoint, but there are also some intriguing rules to bear in mind.

Rule 12 Searching & identifying your ball

There is a two-step procedure involved here. First, you've got to search for your ball. Then, only when you find it, can you begin to identify it. Obviously if you are in the middle of the fairway there is no searching required and there will most likely be no problems in identifying your ball, either. Therefore, this part of the rule book deals predominantly with areas of the course where it perhaps isn't obvious where your ball is or, indeed, whether it's your ball or not.

Above and right: Always help other members of your group search for a ball. It's courteous and helps avoid slow play.

In long grass

You are allowed to touch or bend long grass, rushes, bushes, heather and the like, but only to the extent necessary to find and identify your ball. You need to be delicate here – don't go rummaging around like a maniac – and in the process you must not improve the lie of the ball, the area of your intended swing, or indeed the line of play.

If the lie is really appalling, the rules do permit you to lift the ball for the purposes of identifying it. You can't do this in a hazard, though, and

you certainly can't use the exercise as an excuse to improve your lie, either. It's also very important that before you even touch the ball you first announce your intentions to your opponent or fellow competitor. Then, in the presence of a witness, you can mark the position of the ball, pick it up, identify it (cleaning away excess dirt, but only if absolutely necessary) and replace it in the exact position it was in before being lifted. If you don't follow this procedure to the letter, you will be penalised one stroke.

In a bunker

If your ball is completely buried in a bunker *(right)*, which can happen in certain circumstances, especially when the sand is very soft and fluffy, you are allowed to brush aside as much sand as is necessary to confirm that the ball is there. But

that's as far as you can go. You don't actually need to identify it as your ball, because there is no penalty for playing a wrong ball in a hazard.

If the ball moves while you are brushing aside the sand, or if you brush aside too much sand and thus inadvertently improve the lie, do not panic – there is no penalty. However, you must restore the lie to its original state. It's a two-stroke penalty for a breach of this rule, or loss of hole in matchplay.

PROBLEM SOLVER

What happens if I play a shot in a bunker and then discover it is not mine?
If you assume that a ball is your own, then play a bunker shot on to the green only to then learn that it is not in fact your ball, do not be alarmed. There is no penalty, providing you do not continue to play with that ball. What you must do, of course, is resume your search in the sand and try to locate your actual golf ball. Obviously if you fail to find it within the five-minute time allowance, you must treat it as a lost ball and proceed under the applicable rule.

Above: No good news in this situation, but at least the rules allow you to fish around with a club as you try to locate your ball in water.

In a water hazard

Identifying a ball in a water hazard? No, we're not talking about a full scuba-diving expedition into the lake on the 15th fairway. This is a shallow-water exercise. Basically if you think you can see your ball, or the water is so murky that you think it's there but you're not quite sure, you are allowed to probe around for it with a club. The ball will almost certainly move if your club comes across it, which obviously isn't a problem if all you are then going to do is fish it out and drop under penalty. But if you decide you want to have a go at playing out of the water hazard, a risky option by any standards, you must attempt to nudge the ball back to its original position in the water hazard before you play the stroke. Tricky and, to be honest, not recommended.

In casual water or ground under repair

It would be easy for the ball to move in the process of your trying to identify it in, say, some quite deep casual water, abnormal ground condition, or ground under repair. There is no penalty for this occurring, but if you intend playing the ball from the condition in which is it lying, you must first replace it on its original spot. If, on the other hand, you intend to take relief, you simply pick it up and proceed accordingly. Once again, the penalty is two strokes or loss of hole in matchplay for breaking this rule or for any of the above-mentioned misdemeanours in a water hazard.

Rule 13 Ball played as it lies; lie of the ball, area of intended swing and line of play; stance

The heading alone for this section appears daunting, but don't worry, it's not actually as complicated as it sounds. Let's break it down as much as possible to make it more easily digestible.

You **MUST** play the ball as it lies. It is one of the oldest rules in golf, going right back to the 18th century, and should be obeyed except as otherwise provided in the rules.

You **CAN'T** improve the position or lie of your ball, the area of your intended swing, your line of play or a reasonable extension of that line beyond the hole or any areas in which you are about to drop or place a ball, through any of the following actions:

Moving, bending or breaking anything that is either growing or fixed. This includes immovable obstructions and out-of-bounds stakes. An obvious example of a breach of this rule would be violently to bend, or step on, branches in the process of taking your stance to help clear the way for an unhindered backswing. That kind of strong-arm approach is simply not acceptable. However, you can back into some branches gently if it is the *only* way of fairly taking your stance. There are subtle differences here, though, so you need to tread extremely carefully – both literally and metaphorically.

Removing or pressing down sand, loose soil, replaced divots, relayed turf, or any other irregularities of surface. You can, however, do these things on the teeing ground *(left)*, or in the process of taking your stance, or indeed in the process of making a swing. So if you brush away an old divot in your backswing, for instance, that's not a problem. You can also brush away sand or loose soil on the putting green. Repairing surface damage on the putting green is in itself a delicate subject, though, so that is covered separately.

Hazardous behaviour

If your ball is lying in, or touching, a hazard, you have to be very careful what you do with the club, and indeed your hands and feet. For instance, you can't test the condition of the hazard. So yes, in a bunker you are entitled to shuffle your feet into the sand to secure a firm foundation, but don't overdo it because that sort of overzealous behaviour could easily be construed as testing the surface.

Above: In a bunker the clubhead must not touch the sand at address, nor indeed during the backswing.

You can't touch the hazard with your club, either. That means in a bunker you must hover the clubhead above the surface of the sand at address. It also means no practice swings that cause the clubhead to come into contact with the sand. In other types of hazard, remember that these rules apply everywhere within the boundaries of the stakes

PROBLEM SOLVER

Stones are loose impediments, which means I can't move them, right?
Well, you are right in saying that stones are loose impediments. They are natural objects, of course. The rules state that in a hazard loose impediments cannot be removed from around the ball or the intended area of swing. You can't even allow the clubhead to touch them during your backswing. However, the local rules at most clubs may allow you to move stones from around your ball in a bunker, for safety reasons more than anything else. The thought of a clubhead striking a stone, at some considerable speed, raises obvious concerns. Remember, though, in a hazard you are perfectly entitled to move man-made objects (movable obstructions) such as cigarette butts, empty drinks cans or candy wrappers.

Pro Tip

Above: By all means rehearse your takeaway in a tight spot such as this, but be gentle.

Careful with that practice swing

It can't be stressed enough how careful you have to be regarding the area of your intended swing. One of the most common indiscretions at amateur level is when overhanging branches in some way obstruct the backswing. In such situations, it is not uncommon for some golfers to be seen merrily rehearsing a backswing which knocks leaves off the branches and they just carry on regardless. But that is a penalty offence, an automatic two-stroke penalty or loss of hole in matchplay, for improving the area of intended swing.

By all means rehearse your backswing to see if the branches are in your way – that, after all, is the only way you can truly assess what kind of swing you intend to make. But rehearse it slowly so that you don't dislodge even the smallest of leaves or twigs. That way you won't fall foul of the rules. During your proper swing it does not matter if leaves are knocked off branches. There is no penalty for that.

indicating the hazard. So, be careful when you're in, say, a grassy area bordering some water because that is then just as much a water-hazard as the water itself; therefore you cannot touch the ground with your club.

There are exceptions, however. For instance, if you instinctively thrust out your club, walking-stick style, to prevent yourself falling over in a hazard then, strictly speaking, that does not constitute a deliberate attempt at testing the surface of the hazard. In such circumstances, you would be in the clear and suffer no penalty.

Rule 14 Striking the ball

To get to the heart of this matter and fully understand the rules side of 'striking the ball,' we need first to consider the exact definition. *A stroke is the forward momentum of the club made with the intention of fairly striking at and moving the ball but if a player checks his downswing voluntarily before the clubhead reaches the ball, he is deemed not to have made a stroke.* This explains why nudging the ball off the tee at address incurs no penalty, because there was no 'intention'. But let's look at some other areas of potential confusion.

Above: A stroke must involve a proper strike on the ball. Any sort of push or a scoop is not permitted.

Push or scoop

Circumstances sometimes dictate what you can and can't do and this is one area where this rule applies. For instance, say your ball comes to rest an inch or two from a fence and you have no way of making a backswing. The definition states that the ball should be 'fairly struck at' with the head of the club. But in this situation there is no way you can make a backswing and therefore no way that you can actually strike the ball. If you were to try, you would actually be scooping, or pushing, the ball out of trouble. That is against the Rules of Golf, and will result in a one-shot penalty and the ball will have to be replaced in its original spot.

Dry state

The Rules state that in playing a stroke you should not accept physical assistance or protection from the elements. This means that in pouring rain you are quite entitled to have your caddie hold an umbrella over you as you prepare to play, but once you address the ball the caddie must move away and take the umbrella with him. Equally, if you're attempting a fancy escape shot from under some overhanging branches, you can't kneel on a towel or anything like that. You just have to get your knees wet.

Double hit

Striking the ball more than once is embarrassing as well as costly. Not only do you have to count both 'hits,' you must also add a penalty stroke. As double-hits only tend to happen when you are playing the most delicate of shots, your pain is further exaggerated by the fact that the ball has probably only travelled a few feet – and yet you have to count that as three shots.

Moving target

Playing a moving ball has rather strange consequences. If your ball falls off the tee in the middle of your backswing and you don't have the presence of mind to stop, then the chances are you are going to hit a moving ball. An air shot is the likely outcome, but if you do make contact you are not penalised under Rule 14, but you are penalised under Rule 18 and incur a one-stroke penalty. The key is to be quick-witted and stop your swing before you reach impact. Then you can simply put the ball back on its tee and start again.

PROBLEM SOLVER

Am I allowed to align the clubhead correctly at address for my friend, who has just started playing golf and frankly needs all the help he can get?
Perhaps surprisingly, there is nothing in the rules which prevents you from doing this. The key thing is this: you must move away before your friend starts his stroke. Okay, so that's an obvious one when a full-blooded swing is involved. But there are other situations whereby physical assistance might be offered and there is no need to move away – perhaps holding the legs still to improve someone's leg action when they putt. That kind of thing is not allowed.

Pro Tip

Lofted woods work better in winter conditions

If conditions are terribly wet under foot, and the fairways are soggy and lush, it's always a smart decision to swap your longest irons for lofted woods. That's because long irons are for the majority of club golfers very unforgiving, even at the best of times. Indeed, when ground conditions are less than perfect these clubs become exceptionally difficult to hit solidly. Fairway woods, on the other hand, are much more versatile. The clubhead design of clubs such as a 4-wood, 5-wood and even a 7-wood, make it easier to produce a decent strike – not just from good lies, but also from those damp grassy lies that you come across frequently in the winter months when the fairways are not so closely mown. Not only do you have the benefit of an easier strike, you'll also be able to generate more height, so you can carry the ball further through the air which is obviously to your advantage when there is no run on the fairways.

Above: In lush grass a lofted wood is a far better weapon than a long iron.

Rule 15 Playing the wrong ball

Believe it or not, you don't have to strike someone else's ball to be penalised for playing the *wrong ball*. Your own ball can just as easily be the wrong ball. The rules on this point are mercifully short, and relatively sweet!

Basically, a wrong ball is any ball other than:

i) the ball in play;

ii) a provisional ball;

iii) in strokeplay, a second ball played under Rule 3-3 (which relates to the situation where a golfer is unsure of a rule and thus plays out a hole with a second ball in order to obtain confirmation of a ruling after the round), or Rule 20-7b (which relates to playing a ball that has been dropped in a wrong place, but where no serious breach of the rules has occurred).

Okay, that's clear, then. The most common acceptable excuses for *not* holing out with the ball you teed off with are: i) you replaced it under an applicable rule – it may have been damaged, for instance; or ii) you lost your original ball and have replaced it in accordance with the rules.

The penalty for playing a wrong ball is loss of hole in matchplay, although in a fourball betterball match the partner of the offending golfer is not penalised. In strokeplay, it's an immediate two-stroke penalty and the golfer must then rectify the situation. That means not hitting another shot with the wrong ball and then going back to play the correct ball. This must be done before the tee shot on the next hole is struck, though, otherwise that golfer is disqualified.

Remember, you cannot be penalised for playing a wrong ball in a hazard. Any strokes played out of a hazard with a wrong ball do not count, providing you notice your mistake and take immediate corrective action before proceeding any further.

PROBLEM SOLVER

What happens if someone hits my ball?
Hopefully, not too much of a problem. If someone plays your ball by mistake, obviously the wrong ball for them, then provided you can catch the culprit, you simply replace the ball as close as possible to its original spot and proceed as normal. Of course, there is a slim chance that the person who hit your ball might not notice their mistake, or else they may be too far away for you to possibly know what has happened, in which case the ball is officially lost. That is very harsh, all the more reason that every golfer is careful to positively identify the ball if there is any doubt.

The putting green

It is on the green that you confront 'the game within a game.' The rules for this part of the course only go to prove that the closer you get to the hole, the more treacherous things become.

Rule 16 The putting green

There are some serious dos and don'ts when it comes to putting, and they are listed below. Ignore them at your peril.

You can:

• Lift, mark and clean your ball;

• Repair an old hole plug or pitch mark;

• Touch the line of a putt, but only in the following situations:

i) When measuring distance – for example, in a closest-to-the-pin competition, or when determining whose putt it is;

ii) When placing a ball-marker in front of the ball – not likely since it's far more sensible to place the marker behind the ball;

iii) When repairing pitch marks or old hole plugs;

iv) When removing a movable obstruction or loose impediment, with either your hand or the clubhead.

You cannot:

• Touch the line of a putt except in the situations just outlined;

• Test the surface of the green by rolling a ball or scraping the surface;

• Stand astride, or on, the line of a putt;

• Play your ball while another ball is in motion;

• Touch the green when indicating the line of your partner's putt;

Pro Tip

Perfect pace

If from just off the green you are playing a chip shot and choose to have the flag attended or taken out, which you are well within your rights to do, you are penalised two strokes if the ball then subsequently hits it. So make sure your caddie or fellow competitor is always paying attention before you hit your chip shot!

It's worth mentioning at this point, however, that short game guru Dave Pelz has scientifically proved after years of research that a ball stands a better chance of going in the hole if the flag is left in, as it is more forgiving to the many variables of speed and line. Bear this in mind whenever you fancy holing a particular chip shot.

One final word about the flagstick. Some golfers may be tempted to try to lean the flag one way or another in an attempt to gain some sort of advantage in the event of the ball hitting the flag. This is strictly not permitted. The flagstick must be either left as it is or centred in the hole and not purposely leant either way to make the hole seem bigger.

Left: If you fancy your chances of holing a chip shot, research suggests you are better off with the flag left in.

• Brush aside early morning dew or frost from the line of your putt;

• Wait for an age for your ball to drop if it hangs agonisingly over the edge of the hole *(right)*. All you've got is the time it takes you to get to the hole and 10 seconds once you are there – no longer than that, and no jumping up and down by the hole-side!

PROBLEM SOLVER

Can someone refuse my request to mark their ball?
In matchplay, no, absolutely not. If you ask for a ball to be marked your opponent must acquiesce. It was not always the case, though. Many years ago, as many golfers will know, there was a rule called the 'stymie' which allowed golfers to leave the ball wherever it came to rest on the green, to perhaps gain some form of strategic advantage over an opponent. But that was banned and rightly so; it was ridiculous that a golfer could have his line to the hole blocked by an opponent's golf ball.

Pro Tip

Don't be too nosey

It's worth emphasising again the point about where you stand while others are playing, particularly on the greens because that's where it is easy to overstep the mark. The most common indiscretion is golfers standing directly behind the hole when a golfer putts, in order to watch the line to the benefit of their own putt. That's not on. It's terribly distracting for the other golfer because as they look towards the hole all they see is you standing there. So no matter how interested you are in someone else's putt, stand well away from the line.

If you want to take a look you'll have to walk into a position after the ball has been struck. Many readers might recall on the final green of the 2004 Masters, this is the exact tactic Phil Mickelson adopted, moving in behind the line of his fellow competitor's putt, after it was struck, in order to observe the run of the ball to the benefit of his own subsequent putt from roughly the same spot. It worked a treat. Mickelson holed his putt and won his first major championship by a single stroke from Ernie Els.

Rule 17 The flagstick

This is what every golfer aims for but there's more to the flagstick than meets the eye. It can get you into real trouble. When you're off the green you have three choices as to what to do with the flagstick. You can have it left in, you can have it taken out, or you can have it attended. Remember, if you go for the latter of the three options and your ball then hits the flagstick, you suffer a two-stroke penalty, so make sure your 'attender' is paying attention.

If you are on the green, your options are reduced to two. You can have the flag attended – with the same implications as outlined above – or you can have the flag out. Bear in mind, though, that just because the flag is out doesn't mean to say it's not a danger to your score. It is, and if your ball hits it while it's lying on the ground, you've got a two-stroke penalty on your hands.

There is one final interesting point about having the flag attended. If you are playing to an elevated green and can't see part, or indeed all, of the flagstick, you are entitled to ask someone to hold the flagstick high in the air directly above the hole to guide you to your target. That person can even stay put, holding the flag aloft, as you play your shot – a rare case of generosity from the Rules of Golf.

Right: On the green the flagstick must be pulled out before the ball goes in the hole.

Pro Tip

Check your path

Here's a little practice tip which is not only extremely effective, but well within the rules of the game. It helps you work on the quality of your putting stroke mid-round, which may be desirable if you're struggling on the greens.

While you are waiting your turn to putt, practise your putting stroke along the length of the flagstick . This clear, visual aid helps you monitor very clearly the path of the putter-head, back and through. If there is any crookedness in your putting stroke, the flagstick will give you all the feedback you need, enabling you to make the necessary correction to your technique.

The only thing to point out is that you should perform this little routine well out of the sight of your playing companions, so as to be sure of not distracting them. And, of course, make sure you do not unduly delay play.

Above: This simple practice drill helps train an on-line putting stroke.

PROBLEM SOLVER

I heard about an incident at my golf club where a player refused to attend the flag for his opponent in a matchplay knockout competition. We couldn't believe it. Surely he can't do that?

Oh yes he can. Not that it's going to win him any friends. The other player simply has to make the best job of the putt, preferably with the flagstick out in order to make sure there is no penalty should he hole out.

Ball at rest, moved or deflected

Once a ball stops moving, you'd think its resting place would be assured. Not quite. Anything can happen after the ball has stopped ... and sometimes does. It pays to know what to do when the unlikely becomes reality.

Rule 18 Ball at rest moved

The definition states that a ball at rest is officially deemed to have moved when it leaves its position and comes to rest in another spot. Which, remember, is why a ball merely oscillating in the wind does not constitute a ball moved. Really, the crux of this rule is what caused the ball to move.

Stop thief!

If an outside agency causes your ball to move after it has come to rest, then you may simply drop it as close to its original resting place as you can accurately determine. If your ball was originally on the green, you may place it on its spot. Examples of an outside agency would be a cat, a crow, a squirrel, or indeed any other animal (at some golf courses in Africa it's not unknown for monkeys to run on to a fairway and steal golf balls!). It might even be the greenskeeper out mowing the fairways.

If the outside agency is a cunning or successful thief – amazingly, it is quite common for a crow to fly off with a ball in its beak – then, do not be too perturbed. Apart from the fact that you might lose a golf ball through no fault of your own, you simply replace another ball where the original ball had come to rest and then proceed as normal. If it is possible to retrieve your original ball, simply fetch it and again place it back as close as possible to its original spot.

Be careful

The rules are less forgiving in other instances involving your ball at rest being moved. Basically, if it is moved by you, your caddie, or a piece of equipment belonging to you or your partner, you immediately incur a penalty of one stroke. You must then replace the ball on its original spot and play on from there.

Above: If the ball falls off its tee-peg mid-swing, you need the presence of mind to stop your swing in its tracks, re-tee the ball and start all over again. No nasty consequences, then, just the slight inconvenience.

In the clear

You are not penalised, however, if you accidentally move your ball in any of the following circumstances:

• Measuring to determine which ball is furthest from the hole – a common requirement on the putting green;

• Searching for a covered ball in a hazard, casual water or ground under repair;

• In the process of repairing a hole plug or pitch mark on the green;

• While removing a loose impediment on the putting green;

• While lifting, placing or replacing a ball as necessary in the course of taking relief from an applicable rule;

• During the course of lifting a ball that is either interfering with, or assisting, play;

• While clearing a movable obstruction out of the way.

Ball moving after address

If your ball moves after you've addressed it (other than as the result of a stroke, of course) you are held responsible and thus incur a one-stroke penalty. The ball then needs to be replaced on its original spot. The exception to this is when a ball moves mid-swing and, not having the presence of mind to stop yourself, you despatch it several hundred yards down the fairway. That doesn't get you off the hook, though. You have to add a penalty stroke for hitting a moving ball, and then proceed from where the ball has come to rest.

Danger on the loose

If you are attempting to move any loose impediments lying within a club-length of your ball and that action causes your ball to move, you are penalised one stroke. The only time you can get away with this is on the putting green, when the same action moves your ball or your ball-marker. Each time, though, you have to replace the ball on its original spot before you proceed.

PROBLEM SOLVER

A wobble in the wind!

The definition of a ball at rest moved clearly discounts situations where the ball merely oscillates in the wind, quite common on links courses, and also those times when you just touch the ball with the club as you address the ball (below). There's a lot of confusion about that one, so it does no harm to stress again, providing the ball does not leave its spot you are in the clear.

PROBLEM SOLVER

What happens if a golfer kicks a ball by accident while searching for it in, say, long grass?

Well, it depends who does the kicking. Searching for your ball in the rough is a potentially hazardous business. The good news is there is no penalty if your opponent (in matchplay) or your fellow competitor (in strokeplay) stumbles on the ball by accident – you simply thank them for finding it and put it back in its original resting place before you hit your shot. If it's you who kicks the ball, though, you are penalised. It's a tough break, because obviously you didn't do it deliberately, so it pays to tread carefully when you are looking for your ball.

Ball in motion, deflected or stopped

If a ball at rest can be knocked off its spot when you least expect it, then so can a ball that has yet to complete its journey. And we're not talking about simple bad bounces and deflections off trees. It can get much, much more intriguing than that.

Rule 19 Ball in motion, deflected or stopped

First the good news.

Rub of the green

If your ball in motion is deflected or stopped by an outside agency, then that is known as a rub of the green and you play the ball as it lies. This can work both ways, of course. If your ball hits the greenskeeper's tractor and bounces on to the green two feet from the pin, then you are in luck. But the bad news is that the rub of the green can also work against you. If your ball deflects off that same piece of equipment and over the out-of-bounds fence, there's nothing you can do about it. It's tough. You have to treat it just as you would any other 'OB- situation'.

Animal interference

If you hit a shot and the ball, while still in motion, gets carried away – say by a dog, or a squirrel picks it up and runs off with it (don't laugh, it has been known to happen) – then you replace that ball as close to the spot where the animal first grabbed it and play on from there without penalty. If you're on the green, though, and your putt is interfered with on its journey to the hole, then you should cancel the stroke and play it again from the original spot. Once again, if the thief makes a clean getaway with your ball you can simply substitute it with another.

Don't touch

If your ball is deflected or stopped while in motion, either by you, your partner or your equipment, or indeed either of your caddies, then you lose that hole in matchplay. In strokeplay you incur a two-stroke penalty and then have to play the ball as it lies. If, however, your ball hits your opponent, or your fellow competitor, or their equipment or caddies,

Left: You are permitted to take relief from holes made by burrowing animals. Furthermore, if one of those animals should actually move your ball you're entitled to replace the ball in its original position without penalty.

there is no penalty incurred by anyone – providing it is an accident, of course. What then happens is that you choose either to play it as it lies, or cancel the stroke altogether and play the stroke again. If you take the latter option, you must replay the stroke before another shot is played by either party.

Balls collide

If you hit a shot and your ball collides with another ball at rest, there is no penalty – you simply play the ball as it lies. The exception, however, is when both balls are on the putting green, in which case the player who struck the ball is the guilty party. That's why it pays to ask for the other ball to be marked. Let's face it, hitting a wild putt is bad enough without also incurring a two-stroke penalty or loss of hole in matchplay for a ball strike.

PROBLEM SOLVER

What happens if I hit a shot and my ball then strikes my golf bag?
It's bad news, sadly. You either lose the hole in matchplay or incur an immediate two-stroke penalty in a strokeplay competition.

This is why all golfers should be very careful where they leave their golf bag. It's common to have to walk back from a green to the next tee and, quite naturally, there is no need to take a whole set of clubs with you. Most golfers will simply bring the club they need for that tee shot. That's fine, but just make sure the bag is left safely away from the line of play. Don't take any chances. It's a cruel penalty, this one, because you'll feel extremely hard-done by.

Equally, if you hit a shot out of a greenside bunker and it flies past the pin and hits your golf bag, you are penalised. Make sure you never leave your golf bag on an extension of the line of play; it may cost you dearly.

Relief situations and procedures

If you make a mistake, or find yourself in a sticky situation, you can compound the problem by not knowing the correct procedures. Conversely, a thorough knowledge of these laws can help ease you out of a tight spot in the most efficient manner. It's better to be smart than sorry.

Rule 20 Lifting and dropping

Any time you're thinking about lifting, dropping, placing or replacing a ball you're in a vulnerable position. A moment's impetuosity is all it takes to land you in trouble.

Lifting with care

The only time you can lift a ball without fear of rules retribution is when you pluck it out of the hole. At any other time you must inform another member of your group of your intentions and then mark the position of the ball before you even touch it. If you don't do that, you will incur an

Right: The correct dropping procedure is arm outstretched at shoulder height, then simply let the ball drop from your hand.

immediate one-stroke penalty – not a good start to your relief procedure. If for some reason you move the marker in the process of lifting the ball, then there is no penalty providing you instantly replace the marker on its spot.

Avoid dropping a clanger

The procedure for dropping a ball – whether it's a free drop or a penalty drop – is simple. You stand upright, with your arm extended at shoulder height, and let the ball drop. You can drop it to the side of you or in front of you, but you mustn't throw it or spin it in your fingers – just let gravity take its course. Again, just by adopting an incorrect style you incur a penalty of one stroke, so make sure you do it right. If the ball hits you, either on the way down or after it has bounced, you may re-drop without penalty. The same rule applies if the ball strikes your caddie, your golf bag, or even your partner.

Drop zone

A ball should never be dropped nearer the hole. That rule is set in stone. But what situations dictate whether or not you should *re-drop*? Well, amazingly there are seven possible scenarios where a drop has to be followed by a re-drop. These are:

1 If the ball rolls into a hazard;

2 If the ball rolls out of a hazard – you obviously have to be in a hazard in the first place;

3 If the ball rolls onto the putting green. If you were on the putting green in the first place you wouldn't be required to drop the ball, merely place it;

4 If the ball rolls out of bounds – it would be harsh if you weren't allowed to re-drop under circumstances as unfortunate as that;

5 If the ball rolls back into a position where it is affected by either an immovable obstruction or some abnormal ground condition from which you were taking relief in the first place. Again, that makes perfect sense;

Always think before you drop

That just about covers the key procedures for taking a drop, but there are a couple of other important points to make before we move on. First of all, always call over one of your fellow competitors or your opponent, as it is important for them to be aware of what you are doing. On the professional tours a referee is usually on hand to make sure everything is above board. That won't be the case at amateur level, so the responsibility of being a witness falls upon a member of your playing group.

Also, don't rush into anything. As we will say repeatedly through the many sections of this book, it is easy to let the frustration of having to take a penalty drop cloud your judgement and cause you to do something hasty. Go through your options in your mind and be clear what you intend to do, *before you do anything*. Only then should you take action. Just by pausing for a second or two you avoid the nightmare scenario of adding another penalty for a breach of the dropping rules to the penalty you might already have incurred.

6 If the ball comes to rest more than two club-lengths from the spot where it first struck the ground;

7 If the ball comes to rest nearer the hole.

However, in all seven situations, re-dropping is not a never-ending process. Once you have re-dropped once – that's two drops in total – you must then place it as near as possible to the spot where it first struck the ground. If, for some reason, the ball rolls off into a non-recoverable position, it may have disappeared down an animal burrow perhaps, then you can substitute that ball with another without penalty.

PROBLEM SOLVER

How do you know whether to measure one club-length or two when taking a drop?
Simple, a penalty drop gives you two club-lengths to work in and a free drop gives you just the one club-length.

Rule 20 Placing, replacing and playing from the wrong place

Okay, we're still on Rule 20 – it's a lengthy section, with dozens of very relevant and realistic scenarios.

Placing and replacing

It's best if you are the one who replaces your own ball. Your partner can do it for you, say in a fourball match, but you are the one who takes the rap when something goes wrong – so take control of the situation yourself and save any partnership-wrecking incidents.

At this stage it's worth reiterating a point made earlier. If a ball-marker is moved, or indeed if the ball itself is moved, in the process of marking that ball or replacing it, then you are not penalised. But you must put the

Above: You must replace the ball back on the green in the exact spot where it originally came to rest.

marker back on its original spot before you play your next stroke. Obviously it might be difficult to determine the exact spot, down to the nearest hair's-breadth, but you must attempt to place it as near as possible to what you feel was the original spot. It's a one-stroke penalty if you are subsequently deemed to have got it wrong.

Original lies

The rules are fair and, rightly, you are entitled to the lie you are given, good or bad. If the lie of a ball that you are about to replace is altered in some way, then that is not right. So you can then place the ball in the nearest lie most similar to the original lie, up to one club-length away and no nearer the hole.

If you are in a bunker, then you have to try to recreate the original lie as best you can and replace the ball on that spot. This kind of

Above: A player may have his ball marked, if there is a chance that the lie will be potentially altered by the playing of another shot.

situation can easily arise if, say, two balls come to rest very close together in the sand and one of you has to mark your ball in order for the other golfer to play the shot without interference. That's obviously going to destroy your original lie – either with footprints or by the clubhead splashing through the sand – so it is only fair that you should be entitled to recreate the original lie. Don't use this as an opportunity to give yourself a better lie, though. If the ball was half-buried in the first place, then half-buried it must be before you play your shot.

Moving ball

If a ball won't stay on its spot every time you try to replace it, then you have to use your initiative and find a spot no nearer the hole where the ball will stay put. Strangely, this is not an uncommon scenario,

Pro Tip

Tidying-up in a drop zone

Here's an interesting point that you might want to bear in mind. It could save you a lot of bother some time in the future. If you are in the process of taking a penalty drop, you are well within your rights to remove loose impediments – such as leaves or twigs – from the area in which you will be dropping the ball. This obviously boosts your chances of getting a clean lie. That little bit of thinking ahead can make a big difference to your next shot. In view of the rules relating to loose impediments in hazards, though, you cannot do any similar tidying-up in a bunker.

especially on fast-sloping greens or, say, severely contoured fairways. You should involve your opponent or fellow competitor when replacing a ball, just to ensure there is agreement about what is a fair place on which to replace the ball.

Wrong time, wrong place

Playing a shot from the wrong place incurs a two-shot penalty, or a loss of hole in matchplay. Worse still, if you then don't take immediate corrective action in accordance with the rules you are disqualified.

The real danger situation is when you have to play a shot from the spot where your previous shot was played (an example would be if you have knocked a ball out of bounds) or if you have elected to cancel a previous stroke and play it again (say you hit a putt that was deflected by your opponent's putter, which had inadvertently been left on the ground). The procedures in such circumstances vary depending on where you are on the course.

If you are on the tee, then anywhere within the two tee-markers is acceptable – you don't have to go to the exact spot from where you hit the previous shot. If you are on the putting green, you place the ball as close as possible to its original spot, rather than drop it. And if you are anywhere else on the course, or in a hazard, you drop it, again as close as possible to the spot from which you played the previous stroke. This can be harsh if you are dropping in a bunker, because the ball will obviously plug to some extent, but that's a tough break you will just have to accept.

PROBLEM SOLVER

What if someone's ball marker interferes with the line of my putt?
That's quite a common occurrence, actually. Golfers can use virtually anything to mark a ball on the green, although a small coin is the sensible option. But still, that can deflect a slow rolling ball. So if that marker interferes with your line of putt, you may ask for it to be moved aside. Indeed, you may find that the polite or experienced golfer will offer to do so, unprompted. This can be done by measuring to one side with the aid of your putter-head. Just make sure the marker is returned to its original spot before the ball is replaced.

Rule 21 Cleaning your ball

Don't take anything for granted on this rule. Your ball may have the most enormous lump of mud stuck to it, but don't assume you can just go ahead and clean it off, because in some situations it isn't that simple. Here's what you can and can't do:

You can clean your ball once it has come to rest on the putting green, although you should first mark its location, either with a small coin or other similar shaped object, and ideally behind the ball (not to the side, or in front).

Elsewhere on the course:

You can't clean your ball when you have lifted it in the process of determining whether it is damaged or, in other words, unfit for play.

You can clean your ball in the process of identifying it, if it is strictly necessary. But once you've cleaned off enough mud, or whatever else is stuck to the ball, to be able to confirm that it is yours, you then have to stop right there. You can't go on cleaning it until it is whiter than the driven snow!

You can't clean your ball if you have just lifted it because it interferes with play. This might occur when two balls come to rest side by side on the fairway, for instance. Sure, you can mark and lift one of

PROBLEM SOLVER

What if there's a bug on my ball?
Is it dead or alive? That's the key question you need to ask, for there exists a strange anomaly in this area, the kind that the rules of golf occasionally bring up. A dead insect stuck to your ball, or more likely the remnants of one, cannot be removed 'through the green' – remember, that's classified as anywhere on the course other than the teeing ground, green or any hazard. But a live insect can be cleaned off, because it is not considered to be adhering to the ball. You have to be careful, though, either delicately removing it or blowing it away. You can't lift the ball unless provided for in one of the cases listed above.

the balls to allow one of you to play a shot, but the ball has to go back on the ground in the exact state it was in before – muddy or not.

You can't clean your ball if it's sitting pretty in the middle of the fairway, but has a lump of mud stuck to it. Yes, it might alter the flight characteristics of the ball, but that's something you have to live with until your ball has safely come to rest on the putting green. Then you can mark, lift and clean it.

Pro Tip

A clean ball ensures optimum performance

The first thing to do when you walk on to any putting green (that is, after you've repaired your pitch mark) is mark the ball and clean it. Putting is such a precise art that you don't want anything coming between the clubface and the ball – even the smallest piece of grit on the ball or patch of mud might produce a strange contact and a missed putt.

You certainly shouldn't even dream of teeing off with anything other than a pristine ball. There are ball-washers beside the teeing ground at most clubs. Even if that isn't the case, it doesn't take much effort to give the ball a quick wipe with a towel. Remember, the dimples on a ball are there to aid aerodynamics and spin. It's not going to do you any favours if some of the dimples are clogged up with dry mud.

Right: It is always best to play with a clean golf ball, in order to optimise its flight and spin characteristics.

Rule 22 Ball interfering with, or assisting play

As we mentioned earlier in the book, many years ago there was a rule called the 'stymie,' which basically meant if a ball was in your way on the putting green, it was your problem. You had to find a way to the hole by either going around or over it – hardly what could be described as fair.

Today, thankfully, there are rules designed to provide a more equitable solution to situations in which one ball is influencing in some way the play of another ball. Obviously the position of a ball can have either a positive or a negative effect on you, depending on the circumstance, and therefore there are two sides to this coin.

Assistance

Nobody likes to give away an advantage, so you are perfectly entitled to lift and mark your ball if you feel it will provide some form of assistance to any other player in your group. Indeed, in a strokeplay event you are entitled to play first rather than lift and mark, if you so wish. You do not have this option in matchplay.

Interference

Equally, you do not deserve to be hampered by the location of another golfer's ball. So you are entitled to ask for another ball to be marked and lifted if you feel it interferes with your play. This doesn't apply only to physical interference, either. It can be the mental kind, too. For instance, if you are preparing to putt and find that a ball lying to the side, but not actually on the line of play, is catching your eye and distracting you then you can ask for it to be marked.

Bear in mind, however, that unless the ball is on the putting green, it cannot be

Above: Feel free to have another ball marked, even if it is merely a distraction in your peripheral line of vision.

cleaned when lifted. The penalty for any breach of rule 22 is the familiar loss of hole in matchplay, or a two-stroke penalty in a strokeplay competition.

No funny business!

In theory, two devious golfers in a strokeplay event could come to some mutual prior agreement to leave in place any ball that assists the other in some way. For example, a ball lying 6in (15cm) beyond the hole would be a useful backstop for a golfer faced with a nasty, downhill chip. Don't even think about pulling this kind of stunt, though. If there's proof of this sort of behaviour, it will mean immediate disqualification.

Pro Tip

Take a moment before you hole out

A lot of short putts are missed through carelessness. It only takes a moment, too. Amateurs are sometimes so anxious to get out of the way that they rush their putts and nearly always end up missing. That's not to say every golfer should take an age over every short putt, because there's far too much slow play around these days as it is, but there's a happy medium. Unless it's a real tap-in, it's best to mark your ball and take a moment to compose yourself, time to forget about the putt you've just missed. The other advantage of that is while you wait for your fellow competitor to putt you can look at the break on yours. So when your turn comes around you know the line and you're ready to go.

PROBLEM SOLVER

Is a golfer allowed to claim mental interference from a ball when it is on the fairway. For instance, say I'm preparing to hit a delicate pitch shot to the green and there is a ball on a direct line to the flag, 15 or 20 paces ahead of me. Obviously it's not in the way, as such. But can I ask for it to be marked and lifted?

Yes, you can. If that ball is catching your eye and you think it is putting you off in some way, no matter how slight, you are quite within your rights to ask your opponent to mark and lift it out of the way.

Rule 23 | Loose impediments

Mention the words 'loose impediment' to a large proportion of average golfers and you'll probably be met with a pretty vacant expression. It's not surprising, really, because superficially it is a fairly nondescript term. That's why it is best to refer to loose impediments by their more common term, *natural objects*.

Natural objects means what it says – leaves, twigs, branches, stones, pine cones, apple cores, banana skins, that sort of thing. You might not have known where to look for a loose impediment, but natural objects ... well, they're all over the golf course.

Indeed they are, which is why it is imperative that you know how to deal with natural objects whenever you and your golf ball come in contact with them. The good news is that, providing the natural object isn't fixed or growing and isn't solidly embedded in the ground or stuck to the ball, nor is the object or the ball in a hazard, you can move it without penalty. Be very careful, though. If the ball moves while you're merrily going about the business of moving the loose impediment, you will suffer

Right: It is permissible to tidy up natural objects from around your ball, but if the ball moves in the process there is a penalty, so be careful.

a one-stroke penalty.
You've also got to make
sure you replace the ball
on its spot before you play
your next shot.

It is essential,
therefore, that before you
even consider moving a
natural object from around
your golf ball, you ensure
the ball will not move in
the process. If there's even
the slightest doubt, don't
touch a thing because it's
not worth the risk.

*Above: Loose impediments are essentially
natural objects. Providing they are not 'fixed,
growing, or solidly embedded,' they can be
moved without penalty.*

All clear? Good, because wouldn't you know it, there are some
other, less clear-cut, issues to consider concerning loose impediments,
or natural objects. For example, sand and loose soil *are* classified as
loose impediments on the green and therefore may be brushed away.
But off the green, sand and soil suddenly *are not* classified as loose
impediments and therefore cannot be moved.

As for snow... well, if you are intrepid enough to be out on the
course in that kind of weather, you have a choice. You can call snow a
loose impediment, in which case you can brush it away from around
your ball; or you can call it casual water, in which case you can take a
free drop to the nearest point of relief – which is likely to be the
clubhouse! The same rules and procedures apply to ice. Strangely,
though, the rules aren't so generous in the case of frost – you just have
to live with that ground condition and play the ball as it lies.

Well and truly bunkered

Remember, loose impediments are movable. But not when you are in a
hazard. So if by some misfortune your ball plummets into a bunker
and comes to rest against a fallen branch or some small twigs or leaves,
sadly that is just a bad 'rub of the green.' You can't move the branch –
you have to either attempt to play the ball as it lies or, if that is not
practical, take a penalty drop.

*Above: In a bunker you may not move loose impediments,
although stones are often the exception to this rule.*

As we have said before, though, stones are a different story. At many golf clubs a local rule exists whereby in a bunker you can remove stones from around your ball. Clearly that's a nod towards safety, because a sharp-edged steel clubhead crashing into a stone at 60 mph could have very nasty consequences. That's a sensible Local Rule, but again you have to be very careful that you don't physically improve the lie of your ball when removing a stone from the sand.

PROBLEM SOLVER

Is a divot classified as a 'loose impediment' and therefore can I move it?
Another interesting question. The answer depends on the location of the divot. A dislodged divot, lying clear from its original divot hole, is a loose impediment, so you can move it from around your ball if you want to. Again, though, be careful the ball does not move in the process. But if that same divot is resting in its original home, the divot hole, it is not a loose impediment and therefore can't be moved, even if you feel it interferes with the playing of your stroke.

Rule 24 Obstructions

Here is another instance of a term that isn't immediately obvious. As with the previous rule, things start to make a lot more sense if you call it by another name – artificial objects, perhaps. In no time at all you can think of all sorts of artificial objects that can be found on a golf course. Empty drinks cans, cigarette butts, a bunker rake, a golf buggy or a pop-up sprinkler head – all of these objects fall under the all-encompassing term 'obstructions.'

But within this category there are, in fact, two types of obstruction. Should you come across them on the golf course, the treatment of each is completely different. So let's deal with each separately.

Movable obstruction

Obviously this applies to obstructions that you can physically move, such as the drinks can or bunker rake. Interestingly, the movable moniker still applies even if the obstruction is substantial enough that you have to enlist the help of other members of your playing group.

Above: A movable obstruction, such as this rake, can be moved without penalty.

Right: If the ball moves from its spot in the process of lifting a movable obstruction, simply replace it in its original location.

So, what to do? Well, if your ball comes to rest against one of these, or near enough for it to cause an obstruction, you are entitled to move it out of the way in order to play your shot without hindrance. If the ball itself moves while you're in the process of shifting the obstruction, there is no need to panic as there is no penalty. You simply place the ball back on its original spot.

You can make life easier for yourself, though, if you try to anticipate when your ball might move in these circumstances. This will allow you the luxury of marking with a tee-peg the exact position of the ball before you start to move the obstruction. Should the ball move off its spot, then you are spared any embarrassing confusion or debate about its original position. It's the smallest of details, but this kind of forethought can make all the difference in delicate situations.

If the ball is lying on a movable obstruction, or perhaps even in it, which is obviously quite possible, then you are required to lift the ball before you move the obstruction. Again, though, you should mark the original position of the ball. In doing so you are removing as much doubt as possible. Once the area is cleared, you must drop the ball as near as possible to the spot where the ball would have been resting had the obstruction not been there in the first place. If you are on the green, you can place it on its spot.

In both instances you are allowed to clean your ball when it is lifted. The rules concerning movable obstructions are equally applicable when

PROBLEM SOLVER

My partner insisted in a recent round of golf that he could take a free drop from the stakes indicating out of bounds. His ball was in bounds, but his backswing was impeded by the white stake in the ground. I thought otherwise and stopped him doing so. Who was right?

You were, although your partner could be forgiven for this particular misunderstanding. Yes, stakes, posts or a fence indicating out-of-bounds are artificial objects, and therefore technically speaking are classed as obstructions. However, a golfer is not entitled to relief from these obstructions, even if the post or stake interferes badly with the stance or the area of intended swing. It's a tough break, but you have to play it as it lies or take a penalty drop. And hey, let's face it, it could be worse. Another few inches of roll and the ball would have perhaps finished out of bounds. That's much worse!

your ball lies in a hazard, such as a bunker for instance. Here you are allowed to move out of the way any movable obstructions. Remember, though, if the ball moves in the process you have to return it in the appropriate manner to its original spot. Any breach of the rules relating to movable obstructions carries a penalty of two strokes, or the loss of hole in matchplay.

Left: You are not allowed to move an out-of-bounds stake from the area of your intended swing, nor can you take a free drop.

Rule 24 Obstructions

Now let's look at the second category of artificial object and the necessary relief procedures when you or your ball encounter one.

Immovable obstructions

This definition relates to artificial objects that you can't physically move – such as a fixed pop-up sprinkler head by the side of a green, or the 'tombstone-style' structures on the side of each teeing area giving information about the hole. The good news is that you are entitled to relief from immovable obstructions. And since the definition clearly indicates that you can't move the obstruction, this means that you have to move your ball instead.

Before you can take relief, though, you must first prove that there is actual interference from the immovable obstruction. Being in the way of your ball's intended flight path is not a good enough reason. The obstruction must physically interfere in the sense that it either stops you from taking up your normal stance or from making an unimpeded swing, or the ball is touching the obstruction or so close to it that it represents an actual problem.

Only then can you go ahead and move your ball into the clear, so to speak, and you have to be very precise about where you move it. If your ball lies 'through the green' (anywhere on the course other than in a hazard or on the putting green, not *through the green*, as in beyond the putting surface) then you must find the nearest spot, no nearer the hole, where the immovable obstruction ceases to be an obstruction. Mark the position with a tee-peg and measure one club-length from that spot, marking that distance with another tee-peg, and drop your ball within the confines of the two tee-pegs. It is worth stressing again that you cannot drop the ball nearer the hole and neither can you drop it on the putting green or, you'll be relieved to learn, into a hazard.

However, if you are in a bunker in the first place and are claiming relief from an immovable obstruction (a highly unlikely scenario), you do have to drop the ball in the hazard.

One particular point worth mentioning is the potential grey area that could arise when determining whether or not an immovable obstruction

When taking a free drop from an immovable obstruction, such as this pop-up sprinkler, measure one club-length from the nearest point of relief (above left) and drop the ball within one club-length of that spot (above right), no nearer the hole.

is actually a legitimate obstruction. By that I mean you can't adopt the most ridiculous stance, with your feet miles apart, and then claim physical interference in order to get yourself out of a tight spot that you don't fancy playing from. To get relief in this way you have to be taking your normal stance. Likewise your normal swing must be impeded for there to be a legitimate reason for taking relief; it is no use rehearsing bizarre, wild, looping movements and then claiming an obstruction. That's not legal – and it's definitely not in the spirit of the game, either.

PROBLEM SOLVER

What happens if your ball is lost in an immovable obstruction, such as a drainage pipe?

Well, the precise course of action depends on the presence – or otherwise – of what's known as reasonable evidence. If it is absolutely clear to everyone in the group that the ball is definitely lost in the immovable obstruction, there is no penalty. You are allowed to substitute another ball and then take relief in the appropriate way – in other words, drop the ball within one club-length of the nearest point of relief, no nearer the hole. However, this ruling doesn't apply to immovable obstructions that lie in water hazards.

Abnormal ground conditions

This is an all-encompassing heading since 'abnormal ground conditions' could apply to virtually anything. Golf courses being the fairly manicured areas of land that they are, though, it is actually quite a concise definition which applies to only a handful of 'earthy' scenarios.

Rule 25 | Casual water

Above: You are entitled to relief without penalty from casual water, such as this.

can't see the casual water when you get to your ball, it doesn't necessarily mean you can't claim relief. Sometimes it is the player just standing to the ball that brings the water to the surface – and that's good enough. You can

This is probably the single most common abnormal ground condition, although if you play most of your golf in a region that enjoys more than its fair share of rain you might think it isn't that abnormal.

The official definition is a *temporary accumulation of water on the golf course which is visible before or after the player takes his stance.* A puddle on the golf course is easy to spot and an obvious case of casual water. But even if you

Right: Dew on the green is not classified as casual water.

claim relief for that. Here are some more examples of what you can and can't do when it comes to casual water.

You can't jump up and down around the ball in order to try to force some water to the surface. You must merely address your ball as normal – in other words, fairly take your stance.

You can claim casual water for snow or ice, though, since these two natural conditions are classed as both casual water and loose impediments. Which option you choose to take in a relief situation is entirely up to you.

You can't claim casual water for dew on the ground, just because you think it might interfere with the smooth roll of the ball.

Taking relief

So what are the procedures, then, when you have established that it is casual water? Well first you must look for the nearest point of relief; obviously that means the nearest area of completely dry land, as usual no nearer the hole. Mark that spot with a tee-peg, measure out one club length from there and mark that spot with another tee-peg. You then simply drop the ball within the parameters of the two tee-pegs. Don't forget that you are *not* required to re-drop if the ball rolls up to another two club-lengths away, providing the ball first bounced within

The procedure when taking relief from casual water involves measuring one club-length from the spot where the water ceases to be an interference (above left), then dropping the ball (above right) within one club-length of that spot.

your designated one-club-length area and does not come to rest nearer the hole.

On the green

Previously we've said that casual water must affect either your stance or the lie of your ball. Well, on the putting surface it's a different story, and rightly so given the circumstances. Obviously, the ruling that you can claim relief if the water is around your ball or your stance still stands. However, you'll be relieved to know that the Rules of Golf don't expect you to have to putt through puddles! So you can also claim relief if the line of your putt is affected by standing water.

In these instances you must identify a spot on the green where the line to the hole is not troubled by water. Once you've figured that out, mark the original position of your ball and place it on the spot closest to you where you've established there is a dry line to the hole. Before proceeding, check with a player in your group that the original spot and the new spot are equidistant from the hole.

You can't take a ball from casual water and drop it on the green if the ball wasn't on the green in the first place.

Water in a bunker

As any rules expert will tell you, a waterlogged bunker is one of the least 'fair' situations you'll ever encounter. It's not so disastrous if some of the sand is still showing, although dropping a ball in a bunker inevitably results in a semi-buried lie. The trouble starts when your ball finishes in a completely waterlogged bunker. Then you have two options, neither of which is the least bit appealing.

i) You can drop it in the shallowest area of water within the bunker, which means you not only face an incredibly tough shot, but also the prospect of getting wet. The one upside is that this is a free-drop.

ii) You drop outside the bunker, no nearer the hole, on an extension of the imaginary line between flag and the spot where the ball originally came to rest in the sand. This second option incurs a one-stroke penalty and, as if to add insult to injury, inevitably means you have to chip over the bunker.

Rule 25 Ground under repair and other abnormal ground conditions

Above: Ground Under Repair is usually marked with a painted white line.

Again we're still on the same rule, but this part deals with ground under repair, a condition that you'll find somewhere on every golf course at some time or other, plus several other situations where the lie of your ball, or your stance is ... well, abnormal.

Ground under repair

This is easy to spot on the golf course because it is usually marked as such by a white painted line and/or the letters 'GUR.' Some areas that qualify as ground under repair might not be marked, though – for instance, a hole dug by the greenskeeper, or some sliced turf that has been piled for collection. These should be treated in the same way.

Taking relief from ground under repair is identical in procedure to that of casual water. You must first identify the nearest point where the condition ceases to become an interference, place a tee-peg on that spot, then measure one club from that spot and place another tee-peg in the ground, and finally drop the ball within the confines of those two tee-pegs. It's probably obvious by now, but worth mentioning again, that you *cannot drop the ball any nearer the hole*.

Plugged ball

This is a common occurrence in winter and yet thousands of golfers do not know the proper procedure when a golf ball 'plugs' in its own pitch mark. On *any closely mown* area of grass it's simple. There is no penalty involved. You can mark and lift the ball, clean it if necessary and drop it as close as possible to its original spot. There is no relief permitted from a ball plugged in a bunker though (*opposite*).

The possible uncertain area occurs when your ball plugs in its own pitch mark *in the rough*. In that situation the Rules of Golf do not actually allow you to lift, clean and drop without penalty. However, in the winter months many committees will quite reasonably extend the 'relief area' to include the rough, but you have to make very sure you know your facts before you unplug your ball. These decisions are known as Local Rules and later in the book we cover them in more detail.

Drop Zones

Greenskeepers often designate specific 'drop zones' when unusually large areas of ground under repair interfere with play. Always lookout for these, especially around greens where drop zones are most common.

Wrong green

If your ball ends up on the putting green of a hole you are not playing, then it makes sense that you can't play from there. What you must do is drop the ball to the nearest side of the green, and no nearer the hole, without penalty. This is actually quite a nice break because you'll probably get a perfect lie on the closely-mown apron of the green. One more thing: a practice putting green is also classified as a wrong green so you have to drop away from that, too.

Animals

It is only fair that you shouldn't have to pay the price for the nocturnal mischief of the local wildlife. So if your ball, your stance, or even your

swing is affected by a burrow or a hole that has obviously been made by an animal, you are allowed to take relief from that area. Again, find the nearest point of relief and drop the ball within one club-length of that spot. If your ball was in a hazard to start with, you must drop the ball within that hazard.

Disappearing ball

This one can pose a tough decision, but you and the other members of your playing group just have to be sensible. The critical point is that there must be reasonable evidence to suggest that a ball is indeed lost in an abnormal ground condition, such as casual water or ground under repair. Once you have that consensus of opinion, the relief procedure is really quite straightforward. First, substitute the missing ball. Then without penalty, drop it no nearer the hole and within one club-length of a spot that is outside the affected area, on an extension of the line formed by the flag and the actual point where the ball crossed the margin of the affected area.

Any time you breach a rule concerning ground under repair, casual water, or any of the other abnormal ground conditions mentioned in this section, you face a two-stroke penalty, or the loss of that hole in matchplay.

PROBLEM SOLVER

We had a very strange incident at our club recently. There had been so much rain that one of the water hazards had basically overflowed beyond the margins of the hazard, indicated by the yellow stakes. What would have happened if a ball had come to rest in this area of water? Is it casual water? Or is part of the hazard?
Good question. And an easy one to get confused on. The simple answer is, however, that the water beyond the margins of the water hazard counts as casual water and therefore free relief is permitted.

Water hazards

Water is water as far as your golf ball is concerned; one splash is much the same as any other! But the rules don't see it that way. There are actually two types of water on the golf course – a water hazard and a lateral water hazard, and each determines what course of action you take when your ball goes for a swim.

Rule 26 | Water hazards

The easiest way to determine if your ball has just dived into a water hazard is by looking at the coloured stakes or painted lines indicating the margins of the hazard itself. These should be yellow. The important point to note from the outset is that everything within this border is part of the hazard, which means you can often find yourself on dry land and yet officially be in a water hazard.

Before you can do anything, you have to establish beyond reasonable doubt that your ball went in the hazard. Obviously if you find your ball lying in shallow water, or in the grass bordering the hazard and within the yellow lines, no further proof is necessary. But if your ball is not found, you have to come to a conclusion with your fellow competitors or your opponent that there is reasonable evidence to support the fact that the ball finished in the water hazard.

Above: If you're feeling adventurous, you are allowed to play a ball from a hazard, although you should prepare to get a soaking!

Once that has been decided you are entitled to choose one of the three relief options open to you.

Relief option No.1

If you can find it, you are allowed to play it. That's not so tough if the ball is lying in the grass surrounding the hazard, although you can't ground your club. But it's a whole different story if your ball is submerged. Even if you can see the ball clearly you have to think very carefully about taking this shot on, because even water that is perhaps as little as 3 or 4in (8 or 10cm) deep can make an escape shot very hazardous. You'll certainly get soaked. Worse still, you could easily leave the ball in the water and then you're really up to your neck in trouble... albeit probably only metaphorically speaking!

Above: Under relief option No.2 you must drop the ball on an extension of the line formed by the flag and the spot where the ball first entered the water hazard.

Relief option No.2

Drop a ball behind the water hazard. Not just anywhere, though. You are required to be precise about where you take the penalty drop. What you must do is identify a line between the flag and the spot where your ball first crossed the margin of the water hazard – a point

Pro Tip

Take your time
Having hit a ball into a water hazard it's easy to get a little flustered and lose your cool, especially if you're on a good score, but that is the first step towards making a possible rash decision. And the last thing you need to do is make matters worse than they already are. At times like this you need to be able to think clearly. Compose yourself and run through each of the options in your own mind before you do anything. When you're happy with your choice, announce your intentions to the other members of your group so that they are aware of what you are doing.

of entry, so to speak. Then you extend that line back away from the flag and drop the ball on that line. There is no limit to how far back you can go and you get a one-shot penalty for your troubles.

Relief option No.3
Go back to the spot from where you played your last shot, a penalty often referred to simply as 'stroke-and-distance.' This is probably the last resort, since the punishment is perhaps the most severe of the three. If you've hit your second shot on a par-4 into water, you then go back to the spot where you hit that shot and play your fourth from there. Hence the label stroke-and-distance; add a stroke to your score and forfeit the distance the ball travelled.

PROBLEM SOLVER

In a recent matchplay competition I pulled up my opponent for taking a practice swing in a grassy area within the margins of a water hazard. He didn't accept that there was anything wrong in that, saying that the only thing you couldn't do was ground your club at address and that a practice swing was perfectly acceptable. It actually got quite nasty and in the end I backed down. He clearly took a divot with the practice swing, though. Was I right to say what I did?

Absolutely. You were dead right. You can take a practice swing in a hazard, providing no contact is made with the grass. But if there's any contact, such as the divot you refer to, it's a penalty.

Rule 26 Lateral water hazards

Lateral water hazards are indicated by red stakes or painted lines. This type of water was given a separate definition by the rule-makers, and very wisely so, to cover situations where it simply isn't possible to proceed under Relief Option No.2 outlined on the previous page. You can still plump for any one of the first three options, but the rules also permit you to choose from one of two further options.

Relief option No.4
You can drop a ball outside the lateral water hazard, within two club-lengths of the point where your ball crossed the margin of the hazard – the point of entry *(above)*. That's a one-stroke penalty.

Relief option No.5
Or you can identify a spot on the opposite side of the water hazard, again no nearer the hole, and drop the ball within two club-lengths of that point. Again, a one-stroke penalty applies.

Pro Tip

When to play the splash shot

It's hard to recommend playing a shot out of water, as the risks attached are great. But if you're brave enough and skilful enough, or the consequences of it going wrong are not too painful, it is possible providing the circumstances are absolutely right for it. That means the water must be shallow, no more than a couple of inches, and the ball should ideally be not completely submerged. Also there should not be lots of stones around your ball, preferably just a sandy bank. If it looks like that, try to play it just like a bunker shot. You must not let the clubhead touch the surface of the water at address, or in the backswing. Other than that, good luck and prepare to get a thorough soaking!

PROBLEM SOLVER

What is enough evidence?

You have to be strict with yourself on this matter. Two examples help illustrate the point. Let's say a water hazard is surrounded by nothing but closely-mown fairway and light rough. If you can't find your ball, then there is reasonable evidence to suggest that the ball is indeed lost in the water hazard.

If, however, the water hazard nestles among bushes, trees or tall grass, or round the corner of a dogleg, that's a different story. You really could not say for certain where your ball might have finished. If you saw a splash, well that's good enough, but don't forget that a low-flying golf ball can skim across water. It's all down to common sense and, above all, integrity. If you really aren't certain that the ball finished in the water hazard, then you have to treat it as an ordinary lost ball.

The penalty for not abiding by the rules is two strokes when you're playing in a strokeplay event and loss of hole in matchplay – hardly the sort of encouragement you will want to give to your grateful opponent.

Rule 27 Lost ball; out-of-bounds and provisional ball

It doesn't take long after setting foot on a golf course to realise that there are more than enough opportunities to lose a ball. Too many, it seems, when you're a novice. So after cursing your swing, your ball, your bad luck, or perhaps all three, what exactly do you do about a lost ball?

When is a ball a lost ball?

Well, that's not as simple a question as you might think. By definition, your ball is deemed lost if: **a)** It is not found and identified within five minutes of starting to look for it; **b)** You have put another ball in play in accordance with an applicable rule; and **c)** You have played a stroke with a provisional ball from a point which is either level with, or beyond, your original ball.

Out of bounds

This is usually indicated by white stakes or a white line, but not always. If it's a boundary of the golf course it may simply be a fence, but it will still be indicated as out of bounds on the back of the score card... or at least it should be.

Whatever, out of bounds is a total no-go area in terms of playing a ball. Of course, there is nothing to stop you from retrieving the ball, but you absolutely cannot play a stroke from an area designated as out of bounds. You have to take a stroke-and-distance penalty, which means adding a stroke to your score and then going back as close as possible to the spot from where you played the offending stroke.

Provisional ball

This is what you hit when you suspect that you may have lost a ball with your previous stroke, or hit a ball out of bounds. By playing a provisional you're basically saying 'that first ball might be lost or out of bounds, although we can't be certain, so if we can't find it then this second ball will become the ball in play.'

If you then don't find your original ball within the allotted five-minutes search time, you continue to play on from the spot where your provisional ball came to rest and suffer the penalty. Just to reiterate that point: say, for instance you hit your tee shot and it proves to be lost. Well, the provisional ball you played from the tee was then effectively your third shot. So your next shot is your fourth.

You can continue to play a provisional ball up to the point where you think the original ball might be, but if you play a shot with a provisional ball from beyond that point, in other words nearer the hole, that ball is the ball in play and your original ball is officially lost. Even if you subsequently find the original, you can't play it. You forfeit that right by playing a shot with your provisional ball from a point nearer the hole.

You are *not allowed* to play a provisional ball if your ball may be lost in a water hazard. But any other time you think your ball is a 'gonner' it is positively recommended that you play a provisional, as much for the time-saving benefits as anything else. Make sure you say as much before you actually play a provisional ball, otherwise that ball immediately becomes the ball in play – and even if you find your original ball you won't be allowed to play it.

Finally, remember that you are not penalised if your ball is lost in certain abnormal ground conditions, such as casual water, nor if your ball is lost in an immovable obstruction, providing that obstruction isn't in a water hazard. In these cases you can substitute the lost ball and follow the appropriate relief procedures without suffering the penalty.

PROBLEM SOLVER

There was quite a scene at our club in the last monthly medal. A golfer hit an errant shot and his ball lodged in the canopy branches of a huge Cedar tree. He could see it up there...or, at least, he was fairly certain it was his ball. But it was too far up for him to be absolutely sure. What was the correct ruling? No one there at the time was quite sure.

If a ball cannot be positively identified then it is deemed lost. That's the bottom line. If there is any doubt whatsoever, it's a lost ball. If he can put his hands on a pair of binoculars, though, that's a different story. He could then justifiably claim to be able to identify the ball and he can then proceed under the less severe penalty of an 'unplayable lie.' Who carries binoculars on a golf course, though?

Rule 28 Ball unplayable

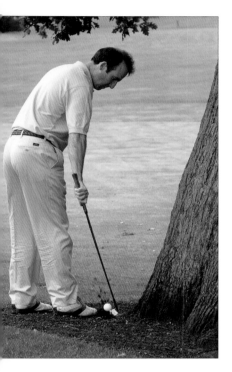

Above: The golfer alone is the sole judge of whether a ball is playable, or not.

Since there are vast differences in playing ability between golfers, the term 'ball unplayable' is a completely grey area. A ball that the novice golfer may consider to be totally unplayable could simply be a slight inconvenience for the low-handicap golfer *(left)*. The key point is this, since the rule book doesn't know how good a player you are it rightly advocates that only you can truly decide whether or not your ball is unplayable. 'Ball unplayable,' then, is one rule which is totally your call.

Putting aside any debates, let's assume your ball has come to rest against the trunk of a huge tree and you really don't like the look of it. The first thing to do is say to your fellow competitor that you are declaring the ball unplayable. What happens next? Well, you've got three choices.

Relief option No.1

First, you can return to the spot from where you played your last shot. This, as you will probably know by now, is called a stroke-and-distance penalty.

Relief option No.2

Second, you can drop a ball within two club-lengths of the spot where the ball was declared unplayable. The usual relief procedures apply once again; mark the position of the ball with a tee-peg, then measure

From an unplayable lie, use a tee-peg to mark the exact location of the ball.

Measure two club-lengths from that spot, and mark with another tee-peg.

Then drop the ball within the margins of the two tee-pegs, no nearer the hole.

two club-lengths from that exact location using your longest club, the driver, for maximum relief, and mark that position with a tee-peg. Then drop so that the ball strikes the ground within the confines of the two tee-pegs and comes to rest no nearer the hole.

Relief option No.3

Third, you can identify an imaginary line between the flag and your ball, then drop the ball on an extension of that line, obviously further away from the hole. Each of these three options involves a one-stroke penalty.

Unplayable in sand

The rules change slightly if you're in a bunker and decide to declare your ball unplayable. The stroke-and-distance option is still open to you, but the second and third options have to be exercised within the confines of the bunker. Which means that you can drop the ball within two club-lengths of the unplayable lie, but only as long as you drop the ball in the sand. And yes, you can drop on an extension of the ball-to-flag line, but again only as far back as keeps you in the sand. Since dropping a ball in sand usually results in a semi-buried lie for your next shot, you need to be doubly alert when considering your options in a bunker.

Water doesn't count

A water hazard is the only place on the golf course where you can't declare your ball unplayable. There is a separate set of procedures for that eventuality, which you'll recall we covered earlier.

Pro Tip

Playing out of a divot mark

Finding your ball in a divot hole in the fairway is desperately frustrating, because your good play has been penalised by the negligence of another. But providing you are not too far from the flag it's not a total lost cause.

The secret to playing a shot from a divot is generating a much steeper angle of attack into impact. Put the ball further back in your stance, nearer your right foot than your left, and make sure your hands are well ahead of the clubhead. This pre-sets the steep angle of attack.

Now you need to pick the club up a little quicker in your backswing and then really thump the clubhead down into the back of the ball. It's a real wrist-jammer this shot, but if you're positive enough you should be able to get the distance you need. Allow for a lower ball-flight, though, and therefore a little bit more run on landing.

Above: If every golfer took care to replace his divots, this would never happen.

PROBLEM SOLVER

What happens if while taking a penalty drop from an unplayable lie, the ball rolls back into the same unplayable lie. Surely you can re-drop, right?
Wrong! If you're dropping from an unplayable lie and your ball rolls back into another unplayable lie, it's tough. You can't re-drop without penalty. You just have to treat it as another unplayable lie. And that is painful, so once again think before you drop.

Understanding 'Local Rules'

Every golf course is different in some way or another and it is for this reason that Local Rules were introduced in the first place. They are designed to take into account, and legislate for, the unique and varying conditions and circumstances that exist at courses around the country. They are not intended to override, or rewrite, the Rule Book.

Often these Local Rules are printed on the back of the score card and in virtually all cases there should be an appropriate list of the Local Rules posted on the notice board in the clubhouse. If you are visiting a course for the first time, or indeed if you're an established member but have never taken the trouble to check out the Local Rules, make yourself aware of them before your next round. Remember, these rules relate specifically to the course you are playing so they inevitably come into play on a regular basis. For that reason they are every bit as significant as the Rules of Golf themselves. The penalties are every bit as real, too.

Hole plugs

All greens are aerated at least once a year, sometimes twice, and for a short period of time afterwards it can create problems for golfers. The turf-and-soil 'plugs' that are removed from the green obviously leave unsightly

Above: A golfer is perfectly entitled to move the turf-and-soil plugs.

holes. But not only are these unsightly, they are also problematical because a ball can nestle in one of the holes, making it difficult for a player to hit a smoothly rolling putt. In such circumstances a committee will often introduce a Local Rule allowing golfers to mark and replace a ball to the side of an aeration hole. Like all Local Rules, it's in your interests to know about it.

Out of bounds

As we've already discussed, these areas are usually marked by white stakes or lines, but sometimes it isn't as obvious as that. Remember the definition for out of bounds – it relates to areas on which *play is not permitted*. But they won't always be marked. An example might be, say, a row of flower beds between the clubhouse and the back of the 18th green. If your ball finishes here you might simply think of it as a tough lie, or at worst an unplayable lie, but that might not be the case. It could well be out of bounds, which means if you proceed under the wrong rule and don't rectify your actions immediately, you are disqualified.

Unusual obstructions

Most obstructions are clearly accounted for in the Rule Book, but some might catch you out. Local Rules exist to help you avoid such misinterpretation. Common examples might be, say, a flagpole, a sleeper-wall around a green, white posts or chains surrounding a teeing area. These objects should all be provided for under the Local Rules to allow golfers to follow the correct procedures. You would usually get a drop from such things if they interfered with your stance or your swing, but don't expect a free drop just because they obscure your line of play. Another example might be overhead power lines crossing a fairway. A Local Rule could exist that allows a golfer to replay a shot if the ball hits these power lines.

Roads on the course

Remember, the purpose of Local Rules is to classify certain areas or objects on the course that might otherwise produce confusion. A classic example of this would be the road on the 17th hole of the Old Course

Right: If a ball comes to rest on a pathway, seek guidance by checking the club's Local Rules on the back of the scorecard.

at St Andrews. Anyone who is familiar with this historic course will appreciate the fascination of the hole. At most golf clubs you would almost certainly be entitled to a free drop from an artificially covered path such as this, but not at St Andrews. Quite rightly, they believe that providing relief off the road would completely ruin the character, charm and degree of difficulty of the 17th. It would become a less fearsome hole – quirky, but devoid of much of its challenge and appeal. So, anyone finishing on the road has to play the ball as it lies. No other road or path is likely to be as famous as this one, though, so unless you're on the Old Course you'd better check out the Local Rules.

Drop zones

These are very easily missed if you're not alert. They mostly exist around putting surfaces, often when large areas of turf are subject to ground under repair making it impractical to follow certain relief options. Drop zones are usually sensibly positioned, thus representing an equitable solution for affected golfers. It certainly wouldn't be fair to put a drop zone in a position where you had to pitch over a bunker, when the ground under repair from which you've just plucked your ball was in nothing like as tricky a spot. Do always be on the lookout for them, though, because they might not always be conspicuous.

Young trees and plants

Obviously it would be insane to spend a fortune on planting young trees, only to then let hoards of visiting golfers go marching into the planted area. The Greens Committee will rightly designate these areas as ground under repair, thus allowing you a free drop out of the newly planted zone. This is one of the rare instances on a golf course where the rules conspire to put you in a genuinely more favourable position than before, as you drop from probably a quite wayward position back towards the line of play. Which is good news for you, but even better news for the saplings. Any young tree that is staked should be dropped away from, without penalty.

Plugged balls

This is one example of a Local Rule touched on earlier. On closely mown areas, such as fairways or walkways cut through rough, you are always entitled to relief from a ball plugged in its own pitch-mark.

PROBLEM SOLVER

What happens if you have a situation where no one in the group is aware of the exact rule? This happened in a competition I was playing in recently. We just looked at each other blankly and eventually took an educated guess. None of us was comfortable with this, though.

Not every club has exactly the same Local Rules. If you cannot get confirmation of a rule in the middle of a round and you are genuinely in doubt as to the correct course of action, the best solution is to play out the hole in question with two balls to cover the potential areas of dispute. You can then seek a decision on the rule as soon as you have finished your round and fill in your score accordingly. This two-ball option is only available in strokeplay competitions, though. You can't do it in a matchplay tournament.

In the winter, though, many clubs will extend this rule to include plugged balls in the rough as well. The only difference is that on the fairway you are allowed to clean your ball, whereas in the rough you will not be afforded that privilege.

Preferred lies

This refers to a committee decision also known as 'winter rules.' That terminology gives the game away somewhat. It relates to the time of year when golf courses are not at their best; a time when greens committees grant concessions to all weather-beaten, possibly frostbitten, golfers.

Basically the rule states that any time your ball is on the fairway, you are allowed to mark it, pick it up, clean it if necessary, and place it within 6in (15cm) of where the ball originally came to rest. It is worth stressing the first step in the procedure; make sure you stick a tee-peg in the ground to mark the position of the ball before you even touch it, let alone move it.

This is all very handy if you don't much like the look of your lie, or if the ball is caked in mud. However, try not to get into the habit of automatically taking a preferred lie unless it's really necessary, otherwise you'll possibly find it a bit of a shock when spring comes around and you have to play every ball 'as it lies.' On the whole, though, this rule is sensible and welcome. Not only can you encounter some frightful lies in the fairway during winter, but it is also felt that preferred lies help protect the course from unnecessary damage.

Pro Tip

Winter rough is tough.

There are many aspects of winter that require you to rethink your strategy and in certain areas your technique, too. One such example is playing out of rough. In winter when the long grass gets lush, usually wet and claggy, there's no way you can hit the ball as far as you can in summer. In fact, you can probably take off at least 20 per cent of your normal yardage for each club. So scale down your expectations and whenever your ball finishes in rough, remember this is winter not summer and your shot selection should reflect this.

Above: Preferred lies is a Local Rule often introduced during winter months, which allows golfers to 'mark, lift, clean and replace' the ball on all closely mown areas.

More problems solved

Throughout this book we've tried to teach by example, highlighting incidents which might easily happen on a golf course and indeed probably already have, as a means of conveying a practical working knowledge of the rules. Let's look at a few more examples of the rules constructed in a question and answer format. To aid clarity, names have been attached to the imaginary participants in this eventful, and blunder-full round of golf.

Flagstick faux pas

Q Fred is on the green, facing a 40ft (12m) putt. Being eagle-eyed and aggressive by nature, he has the flag taken out. Unfortunately his fellow competitor, a vacant youngster by the name of Ian, leaves the flag only a few yards from the hole. Fred is focused on the putt *(right)*, so he doesn't spot the potential dangers awaiting him and strokes the ball towards the hole. But it's too firm – a bit on the wide side, too – and Fred's ball collides with the flagstick. What is the outcome?

A Fred's glum expression gives the game away. He's on the green and his ball has struck the flagstick, so it's a two-stroke penalty. The only upside for Fred is that he can play the ball as it lies, which is nearer to the hole than it would have been if the flag hadn't been there. Small consolation, though, and he wouldn't even have that crumb of comfort in matchplay, because this offence carries a penalty of loss of hole.

Moving balls

Q Dave is in the rough. It's not uncommon, but this is unusual even for Dave because the ball has somehow become perched up in thick grass, several inches above the ground. Unperturbed, Dave gets ready to address the ball and, just as he is about to do so, the ball topples off its perch and comes to rest between his feet. Now Dave is confused. What does he do next?

A That is no problem for Dave. Strictly speaking he hasn't addressed the ball until he has grounded the club behind the ball – that rule doesn't apply in bunkers and other hazards, though. So it's no penalty. If Dave had grounded the club, he would have been deemed to have addressed the ball and if it moved after that point, it would be a one stroke penalty and the ball would have to be replaced on its original spot.

Change of heart

Q Vic has been known to be a bit shaky on the short putts, but things are going well in the final of the summer knockout. He's all-square with two to play and, on the 17th green, nudges a long putt to within a couple of feet of the hole. Mike, his opponent in this final, is at the opposite end of the green and, thinking the putt is stone-dead, concedes Vic's putt. But just as Vic is about to pick it up, Mike realises the ball isn't that close after all and changes his mind. 'Actually, you can't have that,' says Mike, 'it's a bit further away than I thought.' Can Vic pick it up anyway?

A Indeed Vic can. A concession cannot be withdrawn – neither can it be refused. It's just tough that Mike forgot Vic was shaky on the shorties – and it's his own fault that he failed to spot how far away the ball was from the hole. Vic went on to win the match and Mike won't be so hasty next time he thinks about conceding a crucial putt.

Bunker blues

Q Alan's a bit of an ace player from the sand and, faced with a pretty daunting downhill lie, steps into the bunker confident of making good his escape and saving par on this tough par-3. Things

don't go according to plan, however. The slope is severe and the clubhead touches the sand in the backswing. It throws Alan's rhythm completely and he thins the ball into the face of the bunker, leaving him not with the anticipated par putt, but instead another bunker shot. But what's the ruling about touching the sand in the backswing?

A It's not good news for Alan. He is penalised for touching the sand before making his stroke. If you recall the definition of the word *stroke*, it states *that it is the forward momentum of the club made with the intention of fairly striking at and moving the ball*. Well, Alan's swing hadn't got to the 'forward momentum' part, so he is penalised in the same way as he would be if the clubhead had touched the sand at address. Harsh as it seems, it's a two-shot penalty for Alan. Being the unflappable type, Alan at least holes his next bunker shot – even though it is for a five.

Left: A golfer is subject to penalty if the clubhead touches the sand during the backswing, so be especially careful on those awkward downhill lies in bunkers.

Early morning call

Q It's a damp, autumn morning. Trevor marks his ball on the first green and taps the marker down with his trusty putter. Horror of horrors, the coin that Trevor uses to mark his ball sticks to the sole of his putter due to the dampness of the greens. Trevor is a bit slow to react and before he can recover the situation the coin falls off the sole of his putter and on to the green about five feet away from its original spot. The penny has finally dropped... literally, but what does Trevor do next?

A Trevor is in for a pleasant surprise. Since the coin moved in the process of his marking the ball, there is no penalty. Naturally, he must try to identify as accurately as possible where the marker was originally placed and put it back on that spot. Other than that he can proceed as normal.

Wrong side of the fence

Q Pete hooks his drive perilously close to the out-of-bounds fence on the 15th and, being the conscientious type, takes out a 3-iron for safety and plays a provisional ball into the middle of the fairway. Pete's fellow competitor, Phil, walks on ahead and, on reaching the out-of-bounds fence, yells back to Pete that he's found his first ball. It's in bounds after all. Pete picks up his provisional ball and marches forward only to discover that the ball by the fence isn't his ball at all. Pete then discovers that his ball is, in fact, out of bounds. What does he do next?

A It is not Pete's fault, but alas he gets hit for a one-stroke penalty. Why? Because he has moved what had become the 'ball in play,' without the authority to do so. Pete must then replace the provisional ball where it came to rest which, looking on the bright side, is at least on the fairway. Following this situation, Phil had better not expect a drink from Pete at the 19th.

Who's next up?

Q Mark and Alan are playing in the final of the winter foursomes knockout. Things are getting tight and Mark slices his tee shot close to some bushes on the 12th. They decide to play a provisional ball, in effect the third shot on that hole, but are somewhat baffled as to which one of them should hit the shot.

A Alan should be the one to play the provisional ball. Always bear in mind that penalty strokes do not affect the order of play, so even though the usual order in foursomes would require Mark to hit the third shot on a hole if he had teed-off, that isn't the case with a provisional ball.

Hot temper can be costly

Q Steve has been known to lose his cool on the golf course. He's better than he used to be as a youngster, but in the wrong situation you can almost see the blood boiling just below his calm exterior. This is one of those situations. Trying to escape from a nasty lie in the bunker to the side of the 6th green, he takes too much sand and leaves the ball in the bunker. That's enough to trigger Steve off – he slams his club in anger deep into the sand, and takes a kick at some sand just for good measure. Jonathan, his fellow competitor, is worried – not because Steve has lost his temper, but because he suspects a rules infringement has occurred. Is he right?

A Indeed he is. Jonathan has rightly identified that Steve's actions are in breach of rule 13, which prevents a player from touching the sand with the club. That's a two-stroke penalty for poor Steve. But it's just as bad for Jonathan – he has to pluck up the courage to break the news to him!

Mister casual

Q Mark is a casual sort of player, hardly ever taking the game too seriously *(above)*. So when he rolls a long putt virtually stone-dead, he picks up the flagstick on his way to the hole and, with the flag still in his left hand and his putter in the right hand, nonchalantly taps the ball in. Has Mark broken any rule?

A No. As long as the ball doesn't strike the flag there is nothing wrong with doing this, except to say you can look a complete idiot if you miss.

Strange but true

Golf can be a funny old game. Not just funny hah, hah, either, but funny strange, too. Indeed, the game's capacity for producing bizarre on-course scenarios really is quite astonishing. Incidents that might be considered rare, or perhaps even inconceivable, do happen to ordinary golfers around the world.

Here are a few examples that slot nicely into the strange-but-true category. They might not happen to you ... but you never know. They will help you appreciate how a simple understanding of the rules can resolve the strangest incidents imaginable.

Stroke-and-distance, thank you very much

A player hits a full-blooded iron shot which hits a tree-stump and bounces back fully 60yd (54m) behind him, landing right in the middle of a bush. It's now totally unplayable. Of course one of the options in an unplayable lie is stroke-and-distance, which means adding a stroke to the score and going back to the spot where the last shot was played. But in this case that option would involve going *forward* 60 yards nearer the hole, Surely that can't be allowed. Well, actually it can. Even though the player is in effect gaining 60 yards, stroke-and-distance means just what it says, even if as is the case here the distance happens to be of the forward variety.

Sit on the fence

A player's ball comes to rest against a wire mesh out-of-bounds fence behind a green, making it impossible even to rest the clubhead behind the ball, let alone make a backswing. This is an ingenious golfer, though. He grabs his 9-iron and climbs over the fence. So he's now out of bounds. He then takes up his address position, with the fence between the clubface and the ball, takes an almighty swing and hits the fence, causing the ball to hop forward on to the green, only a few feet from the flag. If his 9-iron survived the experience, it would be amazing enough. But even more amazing is the fact that the player did nothing wrong. Anyone is entitled to stand out of bounds to play a ball that lies in bounds. And since the ball was fairly struck at, admittedly with a fence in the way, the stroke is allowed.

Ace ... or no ace?

On a totally blind par-3, a golfer knocks his tee shot over the hill and proceeds on to the green where a ball is lying 25ft (7.6m) from the hole. Not a bad result, he thinks. But ... oh dear. He putts up towards the hole and, as he goes to tap the ball in, sees his original ball lying in the hole. A hole-in-one! But his first thought is one of horror – surely he is penalised for playing the wrong ball. Actually, no. A hole is completed when the ball in play comes to rest in the hole, so the ace stands.

Right: This pike (with a bed spring embedded in its jaw!) was found washed up on a fairway. How it got there, no one knew. The circumstances seemed very fishy, though.

Bad arithmetic

Two players leave the 18th green after a matchplay competition, one thinking the other has won. It is only when they are in the bar discussing the details of the match that they both realise the match was all-square after 18. Fortunately, there's a member of the committee in the bar at the time. They ask him if they can down their pints and head off to the first tee for a sudden-death playoff. No they can't. The match result stands, because there is no indication that any wrong information was given or received.

Guided missile

A player really winds himself up for a big drive, but in the flurry of movement that passes as his downswing, the clubhead snaps away from the shaft. The player can't stop himself and still swings at the ball, but misses it. The clubhead doesn't miss, though, rebounding off the turf and deflecting the ball a few yards off its tee peg. Is there a penalty? No there isn't. The player attempted to make a stroke, fair and square. It was just unfortunate that the clubhead snapped off. He must compose himself and play the ball as it lies.

Index/cross reference guide

All interior photographs in this book are provided courtesy of Angus Murray.

The Publishers would like to thank Brocket Hall Golf Club in Hertfordshire for granting us permission to use the course.